THE LONG RED LINE

THE LONG RED LINE

Cornell Lacrosse and the
Forty-Eight-Year Quest for Glory

Christian Swezey

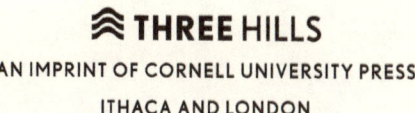

AN IMPRINT OF CORNELL UNIVERSITY PRESS
ITHACA AND LONDON

Copyright © 2026 by Cornell University

All rights reserved. Except for brief quotations in a review, this book, or parts thereof, must not be reproduced in any form without permission in writing from the publisher. For information, address Cornell University Press, Sage House, 512 East State Street, Ithaca, New York 14850. Visit our website at cornellpress.cornell.edu.

First published 2026 by Cornell University Press

Librarians: A CIP catalog record for this book is available from the Library of Congress.

ISBN 9781501790881 (hardcover)
ISBN 9781501790782 (epub)
ISBN 9781501790799 (pdf)

GPSR EU contact: Sam Thornton, Mare Nostrum Group B.V., Doelen 72, 4831 GR Breda, NL, gpsr@mare-nostrum.co.uk.

Contents

1. Via Dolorosa — 1
2. The Pandemic — 16
3. It's Great to Be Here — 27
4. The Wander Years — 47
5. The "21" Year — 62
6. Sprint, not a Marathon — 75
7. Medicine Game — 83
8. The Hurricane — 102

Epilogue — 129

Acknowledgments — 133

THE LONG RED LINE

1

VIA DOLOROSA

Page 52 of the *NCAA Lacrosse Men's Rules Book* states any player with blood on his jersey must leave the game; he may return only after clearance from medical personnel. This was the dilemma facing Cornell junior CJ Kirst, a starting attackman, in the fourth quarter of the 2024 Ivy League semifinal against Penn at Schoellkopf Field. A collision with a Penn defender left Kirst bleeding profusely from the bridge of his nose. Cornell, as the higher-seeded team, wore its home whites, making the bloody jersey more obvious. As a trainer held a towel to his face to stanch the bleeding, Kirst left the field. "I was right there," says Danny Caddigan, starting on attack that night alongside Kirst. "There was blood everywhere." Referees flagged the Penn defender for a rare two-minute, nonreleasable foul for targeting the head-neck area.

The Big Red trailed by two goals. It entered ranked seventh in the nation and as Ivy League regular season co-champions. In the crowded world of college lacrosse, those bona fides alone did not augur well for a spot in the eighteen-team NCAA tournament. Only a victory in the semifinals and another in the conference final would guarantee passage. Cornell needed to beat Penn, and to beat Penn it needed Kirst and his Ivy League–leading three and a half goals per game (forty-five goals in thirteen games). Play resumed about a minute after the hit. It did so with Kirst on the field, holding the ball in his stick, blood still on his jersey. Blood or not, hit to the head or not, he insisted on playing. "I was really frustrated with myself," Kirst says. "The second and third quarters, specifically. I knew I wasn't getting my best looks and was trying to force it. The fourth quarter started, and I got a couple of good opportunities. . . . I got hit in the back, a little cheap shot. After that hit [to the head], I had to show my teammates I wasn't going to quit. I was going to finish out that game, whatever it took."

There were medical issues up and down the roster. Junior Michael Bozzi, a starting shortstick defensive midfielder, broke his collarbone in the second game of the year, a one-goal loss on the road against the University of Denver. He remained in Denver with his parents and had surgery the next day, then rejoined the team later in the week. Because he was injured so early in the season, Bozzi would retain the year of eligibility if he didn't play again in 2024. He opted for aggressive rehabilitation and was cleared to return to practice two days before the Ivy semifinal. If he entered the Penn game, he would lose his extra year of eligibility. On Penn's opening possession Bozzi was there, guarding sophomore Griffin Scane. "I think this [Cornell] team is really good," Bozzi says now. "I knew there were no guarantees. Everyone thought we were in position to make a run."

Junior Walker Wallace, a top longstick midfielder, had the same thought. Wallace broke his foot in late March against Yale. He spent the next four weeks traversing campus with a protective boot and with help from a mini scooter. As the Ivy League tournament drew closer, Wallace ditched the scooter and, for the Penn game, said he was ready to play again. "A little earlier than I should have," he says now. Cornell began with a rotation of two other longstick midfielders. Penn scored three goals. Early in the second quarter, Wallace took the field.

The commitment was there. And with ten minutes and twenty-eight seconds to play, so was the opportunity. Cornell had a man-advantage for two minutes. The two-goal deficit could be made up; Cornell might even take the lead. Ithaca's famously fickle weather—a 1976 NCAA playoff game in mid-May at Schoellkopf Field, Cornell against Washington and Lee, was played in snow and sleet—relented. Many fans wore T-shirts, and those fans were making noise. The game resumed. Cornell turned the ball over. Penn gained possession, holding it long enough for the penalty to expire. The two-goal deficit remained, as did around eight minutes of the fourth quarter. It was a theme, turnovers on offense, lapses in concentration on defense that led to Penn goals. "I remember three times in that game," says Ryan Sheehan, a second-line midfielder, "not even being mad about the mistakes we were making. It was more like, that's not Cornell lacrosse. Something we don't ever mess up, we messed up."

It was a chastening evening. Kirst took ten shots. He didn't score on any. Penn goalkeeper Emmet Carroll made six saves on Kirst, including one with his foot and another with his helmet. It was part of Carroll's nineteen saves overall. Penn won, 13-9. The Quakers advanced to the Ivy League title game two days later against Princeton, winner of the first semifinal in Ithaca. Cornell left the field and headed toward uncertainty. Inside the locker room was study-hall silence. "It was probably the toughest moment we had as Cornell lacrosse players," says

Kyle Smith, a shortstick defensive midfielder. "We went in very confident. The expectation was we were a playoff team, possibly a national championship team. Then we played Penn and they punched us in the face."

For at least twenty minutes, no one spoke, and few people moved. It was past 11 p.m. on a Friday night—the first semifinal included a lengthy weather delay. Cornell's players finally decided to hope for the best, believing the results in other conference tournaments would go their way and they'd play again the following week. "Some of us were more hopeful than others," says Hugh Kelleher, a starting midfielder. The Big Red credentials, such as they were, featured victories over Syracuse and Princeton and one-goal losses to highly ranked Denver and Notre Dame. Cornell supporters, and some players, believed the NCAA would look favorably on having a tournament featuring Kirst. As a freshman in 2022, Kirst scored fifty-five goals and helped Cornell reach the NCAA final. The following year he scored sixty-five goals; the Big Red reached the NCAA tournament, losing in overtime in the first round to Michigan. As a junior he sat in the quiet locker room with forty-five goals, the same total with which he began the night. Leaving the stadium, Kelleher took a long route to walk home, past Ithaca's gorges, still processing the loss. "It's the most upset I've ever been after a game," he says. "I was in absolute disbelief our season might be over. . . . Everyone knew what had happened."

Two nights after the semifinal, on Sunday, May 5, at 9:30 p.m., the NCAA released its men's lacrosse tournament brackets. It did so via a TV broadcast on ESPNU. Traditionally, Cornell gathers in the film room at Schoellkopf Field to watch. Sometimes producers cut to footage of players celebrating as they hear their school's name announced. Cornell's captains received permission from the coaches to move the watch party to the off-campus house of juniors Chris Davis, Wyatt Knust, Danny Caddigan, and others, on East Seneca Street in Collegetown. The entire team gathered. The show started at 9:30 p.m. At 9:40, Cornell's season was over. Its name was not called. The final act of the 2024 Cornell men's lacrosse team was to walk to Schoellkopf Field, roughly two miles. There, the players sat down around the giant red C at midfield and recalled their favorite memories. "We were just trying to brighten the mood," says Alex Holmes, a reserve midfielder. "We were trying to embrace those last moments with the seniors."

The players dispersed for the summer. Toward the end of May, a handful of rising seniors—including Bozzi, Kirst, Wallace, Caddigan, and midfielder Antonio Topouzis—made a quick trip to the Jersey shore. While flipping through the TV channels on Memorial Day, they happened on the NCAA lacrosse title game, Notre Dame against Maryland, being played at Lincoln Financial Field in Philadelphia, roughly fifty miles to the west. "We all looked at the TV," Bozzi says. "That's when it kicked in. Shoot, that should be us. We know we're capable of getting there. We were having a fun time, nowhere near a lacrosse stick or a workout. At least for me, that's when the motivation kicked in. How cool would it be to be with your fifty best friends about to play for the national title, with so many family members and friends in the stands, especially on a day like Memorial Day?"

Bozzi found a picture of the field just before an NCAA lacrosse title game, a giant American flag at midfield, both teams standing at attention for the national anthem, one of them sixty minutes from fulfilling a dream of so many who ever played the sport. Bozzi printed out the picture and put it on the wall of his apartment in Manhattan during a summer internship, then his house in Ithaca. Each day, he looked at the picture and tapped it. "You can get into the cycle of practice, practice, practice," Bozzi says. "And you don't remember what you're working toward. That picture kept me focused."

Others followed suit. Kirst printed out the 2024 NCAA bracket that did not include Cornell. Sheehan remembered seeing an online photo of Cornell leaving the field after losing the 2022 NCAA title game to Maryland. Players were in their "tight-twos" formation, standing shoulder to shoulder in two long parallel lines, like animals marching off Noah's ark after the rain subsided. There are a couple hints the scene in Sheehan's photo is different from hundreds of previous Cornell teams exiting the field. The first is the giant scoreboard in the background, with Maryland's *M* logo over the word *CHAMPIONS*. The other is the one player breaking ranks, the one across from starting goalkeeper Chayse Ierlan; the image captures him giving the senior captain a quick hug and pat on the red helmet. At first, Sheehan swept past the image. "Seeing that picture," he said, "felt like being punched in the gut." He reconsidered. He made it the background photo on his computer. "I thought, why not embrace it? Every time I opened my laptop, it was the first thing I saw."

Throughout the 2024 NCAA tournament, group text messages buzzed and binged when games were on TV: *That could be us; that will be us next year.* Cornell had not won an NCAA title since 1977. For Bozzi, Kirst, Long, Walker, Sheehan, and a handful of other seniors, they had one more chance to end the drought. "We didn't make the tournament, and no amount of complaining could change it," says Knust, the starting goalkeeper. "Like Coach [Connor] Buczek always says, 'The margins are razor thin.' We knew going into 2025 we'd have to do something different."

In the 1970s, quiet locker rooms and missing the NCAA tournament were someone else's problem. Cornell and Coach Richie Moran won the inaugural NCAA playoff in 1971 with a 12–6 victory over Maryland before nearly 6,000 fans in Hempstead, New York. After a couple lean years, in part because Ivy League rules barred freshmen from playing varsity sports, Moran rebuilt his roster. In 1976, the Big Red was undefeated entering the NCAA title game against Maryland, also undefeated, at Brown Stadium in Providence, Rhode Island. On a picture-perfect afternoon, nearly twelve thousand fans filled the stadium. Also present were the cameras and crew from ABC's seminal *Wide World of Sports*. Cornell led by a goal in the final seconds when a little-used Maryland freshman from Suffern, New York, inserted into the game seemingly on a whim, fired a sidearm left-handed shot past star goalkeeper Dan Mackesey. The game went into overtime. On the sideline, Moran's ten-year-old son began crying. "A few of the guys came up to me," Kevin Moran says. "They said don't worry about it, we'll win, we've got this." They were right. Senior Mike French finished with seven goals, the last in the final seconds off an assist from Eamon McEneaney, clinching a 16–13 victory, a game in which Mackesey set a school record with twenty-eight saves.

McEneaney and Mackesey returned as seniors in 1977, and the Big Red again went undefeated, this time winning the championship in a 16–8 victory over Johns Hopkins in the searing heat of Charlottesville, Virginia. In 1978, Mackesey and McEneaney were gone; the Big Red kept winning. It entered the NCAA title game against Johns Hopkins in Piscataway, New Jersey, undefeated. Cornell boasted a three-year, forty-two-game winning streak; it remains an NCAA record. Beneath the surface was something far more ominous for opponents. Cornell's seniors in 1978, when adding their stint on the undefeated 1975 freshman team, and including an unblemished mark in exhibitions and scrimmages, entered the 1978 title game having taken the field sixty-four times in their college career. They won sixty-four times. They were the toast of Ithaca and the envy of lacrosse, with multiple appearances on *Wide World of Sports* and numerous articles in the prominent weekly magazine *Sports Illustrated* and the syndicated *Associated Press*. American artist LeRoy Neiman even got into the act. Known for his brilliantly colored expressionist paintings of sporting events, musicians, and athletes, and at a time when his works filled solo exhibitions across the world, Neiman sketched a Cornell–Johns Hopkins game for a 1977 print he called *La Crosse*. It was available at Hammer Graphics, the famous Manhattan gallery on West Fifty-Seventh Street that once displayed and sold Carl Faberge's Imperial Easter Eggs.

For the 1978 title game, a crowd of 13,527 filled Rutgers Stadium. In lacrosse, at the start of every quarter and after every goal, barring a penalty, play resumes with a face-off. It is the rough equivalent of basketball's jump ball. And in the 1978 title game, Johns Hopkins freshman Ned Radebaugh, five-foot-nine, Baltimore native, with a wiry frame and mound of red hair, a lookalike of Richie Cunningham from the hit ABC sitcom *Happy Days,* won twenty of twenty-two face-offs. He added seventeen groundballs, for many players a season's total. His work gave the Blue Jays repeated possessions, and eventually they found the cracks in the Cornell defense that, for sixty-four contests, had been concealed or nonexistent. Johns Hopkins won, 13–8. Frank Muehleman, a starting defenseman for Cornell, remembers being barely able to talk afterward. "We certainly expected to win," he says. "A friend of mine was there who had gone to Johns Hopkins. He came over and started talking, and I barely said anything. He gave me a pat on the back and said, 'Let's talk later.'"

As the brilliant and flamboyant Neiman divined, lacrosse in the late 1970s largely pitted Cornell against Johns Hopkins, both scrambling to reach the top of a sport with room for only one. It was North against South, New York against Maryland, Long Island native Moran against Annapolis native Henry Ciccarone. Moran was avuncular and generous, with a prodigious memory for names and faces, prone to sarcasm and respond-in-kind commentary. Ciccarone was shrewd and frighteningly competitive, always looking toward the next goal, the next victory, the next battle over a top recruit. Their games were tense and vivid and enthralling, neither coach particularly fond of the other—they nearly come to blows in the 1977 title game and again after the 1978 regular season meeting, and also traded barbs in a 1979 article in the well-known *Sport* monthly magazine. It was a one-on-one knife fight as the rest of the sport formed a circle and held its breath.

Soon, more teams joined the ascent to the sport's pinnacle. North Carolina, led by Willie Scroggs, Baltimore bred and a onetime Ciccarone assistant, led his team to NCAA titles in 1981 and 1982. Next came the arrival of Syracuse. The program was once such an afterthought that, in 1976, Cornell defeated the Orange, 24–6, in a Monday matinee featuring twenty-eight penalties. Moran was so unenthused he dropped Syracuse from the schedule for two years. Less than a decade later, Syracuse won an NCAA title. Its 1983 squad defeated Johns Hopkins in the final, 17–16, after which Ciccarone stepped aside for health reasons.

As college lacrosse broadened its horizons, more metaphorically than geographically, it brought to life a long-held athletic axiom like a playground taunt: Coaches are the biggest copycats. In lacrosse, this meant the targeting of Moran's conveyor belt of hardworking, blue-collar, supremely talented, and largely unknown recruits from Long Island. Muehleman says the only college coaches he saw during his days at Sewanhaka High were Moran, Penn's Jim "Ace" Adams, and a handful from Division III schools. That was about to change. The Long Island players drawn to Ithaca as if by magnet suddenly were much more in demand. "It probably started in 1982 or 1983," says Kevin Moran. "Cornell always got the best players from Manhasset, the best players from Garden City. It was a real pipeline. Then those guys started committing to Princeton, to Harvard, then to Duke."

Richie Moran did the best he could. In 1983, the Big Red ended the regular season with blowout losses to Division III Hobart (by a 15–7 score) and Brown

(13–7). Up next was an NCAA tournament game against top-seeded Johns Hopkins in Baltimore. With eleven days to prepare, Moran and assistant Jay Gallagher held open tryouts for the goalkeeper position. They selected a defensive midfielder named Vince Ilardi, a senior from Brentwood, New York, to start in goal against the Blue Jays. The Big Red also installed a zone defense, a rarely used tactic, and planned for an offense missing leading scorer Bruce Bruno, the 1982 Ivy League player of the year, out for the season with a broken thumb he suffered late in the regular season. In Baltimore, the game was tied at six in the final seconds when the Blue Jays scored the winning goal. "All I can do," Ciccarone told reporters after the game, "is take my hat off to Coach Moran and his squad."

As Ilardi and Bruno, a transfer from Nassau Community College, showed, Moran still managed to pluck a few standouts from Long Island. A couple years later came the son of a veterinarian and Cornell alum in Upper Brookville. Through his father's friendship with Moran, young Paul Schimoler was on the sideline for the 1976, 1977, and 1978 title games. In 1986, Schimoler was a freshman at Cornell and moved from the sideline to the field, as the starting goalkeeper. Schimoler was tall for the position, six-feet-two, and an excellent athlete. Kevin Moran, a teammate at Cornell, says Schimoler was skilled enough to have played attack. Saving shots was his strong suit. "I went against him in practice every day for three years," Moran says, "and I don't think I scored once." Schimoler returned to the lineup as the starting goalkeeper as a sophomore in 1987.

Another Long Island standout that season was Stony Brook native Tim Goldstein, 5-feet-8, 160 pounds, slender with eye-catching speed. He arrived at Cornell for the 1985–86 academic year as a transfer after two seasons, on a rare full scholarship, at Hofstra. There, he initiated the offense as a midfielder. Goldstein enrolled in Cornell's hotel administration school and spent the 1986 season as a redshirt; under NCAA rules, he had to sit out one year after transferring to another Division I program. Goldstein spent the spring of 1986 with the Southern Tier Lacrosse Club, sponsored by Royal Motors of Cortland—"proudly serving the Dryden, Ithaca and Marathon areas"—competing for the Empire Division championship against opposition like the Niagara University club team and postcollegiate clubs from Rochester, Syracuse, and the Iroquois Nation. Those rosters were dotted with former standouts from Syracuse, Cornell, Cortland State, and Hobart; the Sunday afternoon games were a good proving ground. "Cornell really didn't have much in the way of a fall program back then, so it wasn't clear at that point how good he was," says Andy Phillips, a Cornell lacrosse alum and STLC teammate of Goldstein. "Then we saw Tim play in the club league that spring. He was our best player."

Goldstein's first game with Cornell was the season opener of 1987 against Division III power Cortland State. In a 17–5 victory, Goldstein finished with seven assists, one away from a school record. Later came the trip to the Carrier Dome to face Syracuse. The previous year, not even Schimoler could halt Syracuse in a 22–7 loss. In 1987, with Goldstein in tow, the Big Red crushed the Orange, 19–6; Goldstein provided a program-record nine assists. "The one difference," Syracuse Coach Roy Simmons told reporters, "was Goldstein." Cornell entered the NCAA tournament undefeated in 11 games; the attackman entered as the leading scorer in the nation, with fifty-seven assists. The winning streak reached twelve entering an NCAA semifinal rematch against Syracuse at Rutgers Stadium. Richie Moran, famously superstitious, insisted that if the winning streak held, the same bus driver had to transport the squad. The driver, a recovering alcoholic with a deep, gravelly voice, often began and ended long drives by grabbing the internal microphone and intoning a chant of "go, Red, go!" During a timeout at a crucial juncture of the semifinal, Moran ceded control of the huddle for the exuberant driver to give his trademark call to arms. The Big Red won, 18–15.

The title game came two days later—and just as a few years earlier, it was undefeated Cornell against underdog Johns Hopkins at Rutgers Stadium. A crowd of 17,077, many of whom, in the words of a local writer, "participated in one of one of Piscataway's better traffic jams," eventually filled the stands. Cornell wore its classic white jerseys, with red *Cornell* across the chest and *Lacrosse* running down the side, like a misshapen letter *L*. In the final two minutes, the game was tied at ten when Johns Hopkins senior Craig Bubier had a breakaway against Schimoler. Twice earlier, Bubier bore in on Schimoler with a near-certain goal, only to be denied by Schimoler's quick reflexes. The matchup was the distillation of Cornell against Johns Hopkins, Schimoler from St. Mary's–Manhasset High against Bubier from St. Mary's–Annapolis. This time, Bubier waited until the last second to fire a ten-yard shot to Schimoler's off-stick side. It went into the goal for an 11–10 lead. With thirty-seven seconds to play, the Blue Jays were called for a penalty. Cornell went to its "51" extra-man offense. Goldstein, the leading scorer in the nation, and with a school-record seventy-three assists, fired a pass into the middle of the field; defenders tipped it away. The game ended. Joyful Johns Hopkins players stormed the field as Goldstein, in frustration, threw his stick over the goal. Goldstein finished the three-game playoffs with twenty-five points, tying an NCAA record, yet found little solace. "I'd trade [the points] for a title," he told reporters after the game. "That's what is important."

In 1988, with Goldstein and Schimoler together for one more year, Cornell again reached the semifinals in Syracuse. In its Thursday editions, the *Ithaca Journal* helpfully reminded fans the Cornell tailgate was set for the large tent on Hendricks Field, near the Carrier Dome. On Saturday, May 28, those fans had plenty to celebrate. In one part of the second half, Schimoler and the defense held Virginia to one for thirty shooting. Cornell won, 17–6. Up next came the title game against the host Orangemen and their twin brother tandem of Paul and Gary Gait. Gary entered the title game with sixty-eight goals, near an NCAA single-season record, and eighty groundballs. His brother scored forty-five goals and added sixty groundballs. The numbers were made even more staggering because as midfielders, they played in a rotation, meaning they were on the field for roughly two-thirds of their team's possessions. Moreover, they were only sophomores. In the pages of *Sports Illustrated* earlier in the spring, Simmons compared Gary Gait to Jim Brown, the NFL Hall of Fame running back who, in the spring of 1957, in the lower-scoring era of wooden sticks and ironclad defense, averaged four goals per game in leading Syracuse lacrosse to an undefeated season. "Gary may be as good as Big Jim," Simmons said, "and Paul is as good as Gary."

On Memorial Day 1988, Syracuse jumped to an 8–1 lead and won, 13–8. The sport's Flying Wallendas did not disappoint: Gary Gait finished the season with seventy goals, an NCAA record, and eighty-six groundballs. His twin brother also scored twice against the Big Red, his 46th and 47th goals. "In 1987 I thought we should have won," says Joe Lizzio, Cornell's face-off specialist and a reserve midfielder. "In 1988 we were much thinner talent-wise and depth-wise. The Gait brothers were just too much, we couldn't run with them." For the next two seasons Simmons was an equal measure carnival barker and coach. Come see the twins with linebacker size, running-back speed, sleight-of-hand stick skills and shots that exceed ninety miles per hour. In their final three years of college, they lost one game. As the Gait brothers left the field for the last time on Memorial Day 1990, parading the NCAA trophy, the Big Red title drought reached twelve years.

The 1990s once again saw a dominant lacrosse team emerging from the Ivy League, but this time it was not Cornell. Princeton's new coach bore some resemblance to Moran. Bill Tierney graduated from a public high school on Long Island, as did Moran. They were familiar with the sport's bluebloods, Moran from his days as a midfielder at Maryland, Tierney from his stint as an assistant at Johns Hopkins. Both impressed on their players quitting can become a habit and so can winning. Both portrayed a deep confidence, practically willing their teams to emulate it. And both believed, strongly, practice should be harder than games. For Moran this meant punishing physical conditioning, a truism cemented during his stint in the marines. During the monotonous afternoons inside Schoellkopf Field, players who dropped too many passes or were caught not paying attention heard from their coach the letters "E-G, E-H, E-K, E-L!" The cryptic semaphore immediately sent chills down the spine, for Moran was telling the offending player or players, and sometimes the whole team, to enter the Schoellkopf seating area and run up section EG, down section EH, up section EK and down section EL before resuming practice. (In later years, Moran shortened it to "G, H, K L!") It was not a random selection: Moran picked the four highest points of the Crescent stands. The players often had to navigate ice and snow as they ran. At Princeton, Tierney preached perfection and attention to detail, often repeating a drill several times because it was very good but not quite perfect. This was done, again and again, as Tierney's voice rose a few octaves at each imperfection.

One other shift benefited Tierney—the change in the recruiting landscape. For years, Moran was known for dropping in on the guidance counselor's office at a high school on Long Island and asking to visit with the top lacrosse players. Through his internecine contacts, he knew who to ask about, how good they were in high school, and their chances of being viewed favorably by Cornell's admissions office. Recruiting elsewhere on Long Island was haphazard at best. Many high school coaches simply posted letters from college programs on a bulletin board in the locker room. Anyone interested in the school was encouraged to reach out directly.

In the late 1980s, Tierney joined two other college coaches and instituted a summer initiative called the Top 205 Camp. The best rising seniors in the nation, with recommendations from their high school coaches, were invited to four days of drills and scrimmages in front of dozens of college coaches. Once the high school coach recommendation landed, players were chosen on a first-come, first-served basis. Within a few years, what began with only 205 invites turned into 250, then more than 300, then expanded across a second session. By the mid-1990s, *The Baltimore Sun* reported the camps attracted roughly 600 high schoolers and 90 college coaches. Tierney and others could see the top players for themselves and meet them and their parents, all without changing location, usually Loyola College in Baltimore. Beating down the bushes for recruits became an anomaly. "Recruiting changed," says Greg Raschdorf, who played for Moran in the late 1970s and spent two years as an assistant at Princeton under Tierney. "And Princeton was right there. It wasn't the guidance counselor's office anymore. Now it was a home visit, dinner with the recruit and his family. At Cornell, I don't think my parents met Richie until I arrived on campus."

The top of Ivy League lacrosse did not turn overnight. When Tierney arrived at Princeton in 1988, Cornell had won twenty in a row in the series, and Schimoler and Goldstein were in their prime. That year Cornell thumped the Tigers, 21–5. On April 28, 1990, inside historic Palmer Stadium, Princeton beat Cornell, 14–6, snapping the twenty-two-year losing streak. The Tigers team captain was thrilled. "We outplayed them, outcoached them, out-scouted them," Paul DiBello told *The Trenton Times*. "I can't begin to describe the feeling I have now." For their meeting in 1992, nearly 4,000 fans flocked to Palmer Stadium. Underdog

Cornell led by two goals with three minutes to play. On the sideline, Tierney later acknowledged he didn't think his team would win. The Tigers clawed back and sent the game to sudden-death overtime. The Big Red gained possession first but turned the ball over. Princeton senior Andy Moe ended the proceedings with a goal that gave the Tigers a share of their first Ivy League title in twenty-five years. One Princeton player recalled their coach's brash comment years earlier. "Coach Tierney promised us four years ago, this day would come," starting defender Mike Mariano told *The Trenton Times*. "We believed in him." Raschdorf, living in New Jersey and a volunteer assistant on the 1992 Princeton team, quickly swapped out his black-and-orange sideline gear for Cornell red and hosted a postgame tailgate party in the parking lot for his college friends and their families. Using his expertise from his days as a student at the Hotel Administration School, Raschdorf put together a brilliant assortment of food and drinks. With the party in full swing, he snuck off briefly, went back inside Palmer Stadium, and began sobbing. Raschdorf knew Cornell had been supplanted atop the Ivy League and was not likely to return under Moran. "The 1990 game was the changing of the guard," he says. "In '92, Cornell played their hearts out. I wrote Richie a three-page letter after the game. It was very emotional." Moe scored another overtime goal later in the spring of 1992, at Franklin Field, home of Penn athletics. This goal did not come in Ivy League play. It came on Memorial Day, in the NCAA title game against Syracuse, and gave the Tigers their first national title. A few weeks later Raschdorf quietly left the Princeton program. Though he remained involved in lacrosse for more than two decades and keeps in touch with Tierney, Raschdorf never again coached at the college level.

The Tigers claimed further NCAA crowns in 1994, 1996, and 1997. Cornell went the opposite direction; in those years the Big Red finished 1–10, 3–11, and 3–11 again. In late July 1997, Richie Moran retired. He was sixty years old and accepted a position as a fundraiser for Cornell's athletic department. In 29 seasons, Moran won 257 games and 3 NCAA titles and won or shared 15 Ivy League titles. His last NCAA tournament victory was the 1988 semifinal against Virginia. On the night his retirement was announced, the sports editor at *The Ithaca Journal* asked him about his career, if the recent losses overshadowed all the victories. Moran, as ever, opted for optimism. "I just tried to make my team better every day," he said. "Every day was a bright day."

It would be years before Cornell again threatened on the national scene. In the early 2000s, a sophomore at Hewlett High on Long Island named Max Seibald first turned heads as a midfielder. As a senior in 2005, Seibald grew to 6-feet-2, 220 pounds; finished with 49 goals and 30 assists; and won 80 percent of his face-offs. To that he added a 4.0 grade-point average and SAT scores that exceeded

1400. On his visit to Ithaca, then-Coach Jeff Tambroni made no promises about playing time nor publicity. "You're going to have to work every day to earn your spot," Tambroni told the star player, as Seibald recalled years later in an interview with Cornell athletics. Seibald added, "That sold me and got my competitive juices flowing." His selection of Cornell over every major program including Princeton was a major breakthrough.

As a sophomore in April 2007, one of Seibald's shots in a win over Brown was so forceful it tore the goal net. Weeks later, the Big Red was undefeated entering an NCAA semifinal against Duke in Baltimore. A crowd of 52,004 settled into M&T Bank Stadium. In the opening minute, Seibald, racing from defense to offense near the team benches, was blindsided by a high hit from a Duke defender. He fell to the ground on all fours as trainers raced onto the field. Referees deemed the hit egregious enough to assess a rare two-minute penalty as trainers continued their work on the ailing Seibald. He left the field and later returned to the game, but he was clearly hampered.

Duke led 10–3 in the fourth quarter when Cornell closed the deficit to six goals, then five, then four. The Cornell cheering section began to believe. Senior David Mitchell, a nonpareil inside shooter from Canada, scored his fourth goal and cut the deficit to 10–7. Duke scored; eight seconds later, Cornell answered. The Big Red battled to tie the game at eleven on a goal by senior Brian Clayton, a reserve midfielder, with seventeen seconds left. Duke won the ensuing face-off and, with three seconds left, scored the winning goal. Seibald finished with no goals and one assist. It was this game, and the comeback, that prompted Jon Gordon to begin his research for what would become the hugely successful 2015 book *The Hard Hat*, the proceeds of which go to charity.

The Big Red again reached the NCAA semifinals in 2009 in Foxborough, Massachusetts. The winner of the Cornell-Virginia game faced the winner of the first semifinal between Syracuse and Duke. A crowd of 36,594 filled Gillette Stadium. Before leaving the Boston Hilton Park Plaza for the stadium, Tambroni gave the team a message: Dream big, act small. No need for home-run plays. Be confident, hit singles, believe in yourselves and our system. As Cornell left its hotel, Duke and Syracuse were inside the stadium preparing for the first semifinal. Duke's team left its locker room and ran into a couple Syracuse players stretching in the hallway underneath the stands. The Duke players yelled and screamed as they walked past, their calls echoing off the concrete hallways in the tight quarters. In reply, the two Orange players turned to each other and smirked. Syracuse, the ultimate playoff machine, defending NCAA champs, wasn't about to be intimidated. The Orange led 8–4 at halftime and 14–6 at the end of the third quarter en route to a perfunctory 17–7 victory.

In the second semifinal, Cornell looked even more impressive in dispatching top-seeded Virginia 15–6. The Central New York rivals met on Memorial Day for the national title. This time the crowd swelled to nearly forty-two thousand. Tambroni's team very much resembled that of Moran's heyday. There was a strong Long Island presence: Seibald, a senior, USILA player of the year, Tewaaraton Trophy winner, first-team all-American midfielder, with his twenty-six goals, ten assists, and forty-one groundballs; do-everything running mate John Glynn, from Lindenhurst, a senior and face-off specialist who added twenty goals and ninety-six groundballs; and Ivy League freshman of the year Rob Pannell, from Smithtown, an attackman with twenty-four goals and forty-one assists. The inside finisher was not from Canada per se, as in 1971 and 1976. Junior Ryan Hurley, from Eagan, Minnesota, with a hockey background, entered the title game with forty-four goals and shooting better than 40 percent. Also typical of a Moran team, Cornell boasted players doing double duty. Seibald was the leader on offense and took face-off wings. Glynn was face-off-specialist-cum-first-line-midfielder.

Another busybody was freshman Roy Lang. A native of Mill Valley, California, near San Francisco, he set off a breathless recruiting battle among the Ivy League schools given his 6-feet-3, 205-pound frame; his 155 career goals in high school, including 77 as a junior and 74 as a senior; his excellence in the classroom (at Cornell was a double major, history and American studies); and his athleticism. Cornell won his services and immediately put him to triple duty as a top shortstick defensive midfielder, face-off wing, and anchor of the second offensive midfield line. In the NCAA tournament, Lang added a fourth responsibility, outside shooter on extra-man offense.

Perfect weather greeted the 2009 title game, sunny and seventy degrees, low humidity. Cornell took the field and formed a circle around Seibald, the program's first lone captain since 1965. "This is what we've been working for all year," Seibald told his teammates, with a hint of Long Island accent. "We've got one job to do. And we're going to do it together and be Division I national champions!" The Big Red, eyeing a first NCAA title since 1977, followed up their captain's words; midway through the fourth quarter a goal by Seibald gave Cornell an 8–6 lead. Syracuse won the ensuing face-off, but Lang scooped a groundball and cleared it. Around a minute later, Lang, a newbie to the sport's biggest stage and guarded by the best long stick midfielder in lacrosse, scored on a sidearm lefty shot. The Big Red led 9–6 with five minutes, thirty-one seconds remaining. The thirty-two-year national title drought was nearly over. Syracuse called a time-out. Even the public address announcer sensed Cornell was on the verge of a title, as he chose the break in action to remind celebrating fans not to run onto the field after the game.

When play resumed, Syracuse went into desperation mode, and Cornell, with its smaller roster and double and triple workloads, began to feel the effects of playing twice in three days. The Cornell defense was a step slow to one of Syracuse's inside finishers, and he scored to close the deficit to 9–7 with around 3:30 to play. The Orange won the ensuing face-off. Cornell forced a loose ball, but the Orange regained possession, and two quick passes later, a player was wide open in front of the goal, again a step ahead of the tiring defense. He scored to close the deficit to 9–8 with roughly two and a half minutes to go. Now Cornell called a time-out.

The Orange, still trailing by a goal, took possession in the final minute. The Big Red sent out the starting defense and longstick midfielder plus, as the two required shortsticks, Seibald and Lang. The Orange took a close bounce shot that went wide. Then an errant pass by senior Kenny Nims sailed out of bounds. Cornell ball, twenty-eight seconds left, still leading by one. Seibald took possession and passed to a longstick. The Orange, desperate for the ball and a chance to tie the game, swarmed him. The clock clicked to twenty seconds, then fifteen. Still Cornell led; still Cornell had possession. Then, near midfield, Nims forced a loose ball. In the scrum, Lang noticed something almost certainly missed by everyone in the crowd of 41,935 and many of the players and coaches—Nims, rather than joining the fight for the loose ball, sprinted toward the goal. If Syracuse gained possession he'd have a wide-open shot. Lang raced toward the danger just as Orange midfielder Matt Abbott controlled the ball. Or mostly controlled it. As he lost his balance amid pressure from defenders, Abbott flipped a one-handed, over-the-shoulder, looping pass toward Nims. Lang stretched every sinew of his body to deflect the ball. He nearly did, nearly swatted it to safety and Cornell's first title since 1977. Instead, the ball tipped off the top of his stick and went to Nims, who shot and scored to tie the game with four and a half seconds left. Cornell won the opening face-off of overtime on a groundball by Glynn but lost possession. Roughly a minute later the game was over, the Orange scoring a goal on a close shot for a 10–9 victory. "This is gut-wrenchingly similar to the [2007] loss to Duke," Cornell star defender Matt Moyer told reporters. "Four seconds away," added Seibald, fighting back tears. "There's a lot of emotion in that locker room right now."

Years later, Richie Moran took a visitor through the Statler Hotel, Cornell's jewel of on-campus accommodation. He spied a picture of Glynn, red helmet, red number 20 jersey, and red shorts. "It's a great picture," he said, "but I wish they'd change it. It's from the title game we lost in '09 in Foxborough. Better to have a picture from a game we won." He wasn't the only one. His son, also present in Foxborough that day, says he has never rewatched a second of the game on replay nor highlights. If it pops up on television, he looks away. The Foxborough loss remained ingrained in the Big Red psyche. Cornell reached Championship Weekend again in 2010 and 2013 and the quarterfinals in 2018 but did not win the title. Entering the 2020 season, the drought was forty-three years long.

Tom LaFalce, Cornell alum, standout high school player on Long Island in the late-1980s, later a referee for Moran's practices, has provided color analysis for Cornell lacrosse on the radio and television for more than twenty years. He, too, was in attendance in Foxborough for the 2009 title game and many other NCAA tournament losses along the way. "There were so many close calls," he says. "It wasn't like Cornell was getting to the title game and getting blown out. Cornell was right there. . . . There were so many 'what if's.' I remember calling games and thinking, one of these teams is going to break through. I'm not sure which one, but when it happens, I'm sure as heck going to be there."

2

THE PANDEMIC

Two of Cornell's NCAA titles came with a huge assist from Canada. In 1971, as the rest of the Ivy League lacrosse rosters featured three Canadians combined, senior attackman Alan Rimmer from Long Branch, Ontario, scored six goals in the 12–6 championship win over Maryland. In the 1976 title game, Mike French, from St. David's, Ontario, scored seven goals. (The following year, Maryland coach Buddy Beardmore welcomed his first recruits from Canada, brothers Wayne and Ron Martinello, born less than a year apart in Windsor, Ontario.) The relationship in part is because Ithaca is around 240 miles from Toronto, a manageable drive. It is so entrenched regular season games at Schoellkopf Field include renditions of the US national anthem and "O, Canada." The relationship dates from the 1960s and Ned Harkness. His double duty at Cornell was hockey coach and lacrosse coach. He led Cornell hockey to the NCAA title in 1967 and 1970. In lacrosse, his final three teams—1966, 1967, 1968—went a combined 35–1.

The Big Red entered the 2020 season with a Canadian attackman on par with Rimmer and French. Senior Jeff Teat arrived in Ithaca from Brampton, Ontario, having attended Hill Academy outside Toronto. As a senior in 2016, against the Team USA Under-19 developmental squad, he scored eight goals in a surprise 16–11 victory. *Lacrosse Magazine* wrote that his goals that day "defy brief description." Hill finished 11-0, and because all of its games were against teams in the United States, one poll ranked it number one, expanding its definition to include North American high schools rather than just those in the United States. In Hill's eleven games, Teat had thirty-five goals and forty assists and led victories over the teams that finished ranked numbers four, five, six, and ten. In a testament to his lacrosse intelligence, Teat also was part of Hill's man-down defense, where he picked up a longstick, threw checks, and helped clog passing lanes. *Inside Lacrosse* magazine ranked Teat the number-one incoming recruit in the nation. Tom LaFalce says Teat was one of the most talented players in program history. "Jeff Teat did things I never saw before," LaFalce says. "His vision was unbelievable, his ability to find the open guy."

Teat's arrival in Ithaca did not disappoint. In 2017, he set Cornell's scoring record for freshmen, at seventy-two points (thirty-three goals, thirty-nine assists). As a sophomore in 2018, he led the Big Red to the NCAA tournament and a first-round game at Syracuse. Teat was such a threat the Orange used its best defender to face-guard him. Essentially, Nick Mellen followed Teat wherever he went on the field, facing Teat and turning his back on the other action. The tactic was a success in that Teat had no goals and one assist and took only one shot. It also took Syracuse's best defender away from helping any of his teammates, and Cornell won the game on a goal by reserve attackman Colton Rupp, a senior from Bethesda, Maryland. In the quarterfinals, Maryland borrowed the face-guarding tactic but used its third-best defenseman on Teat. As Jesse Dougherty wrote in *The Washington Post*, Teat had two shadows that day—his own and that of Jack Welding, a senior defender from Southlake, Texas. Teat finished with two assists, no goals, and only one shot. The Terrapins won, 13–8. Teat finished the year with sixty-two assists, nearly a school record, and was named first-team all-American.

In 2019, the Big Red lost in the Ivy League semifinals, missed the NCAA tournament, and finished 10–5. Teat finished with thirty-four goals and thirty-six assists and slipped to second team all-American. The 2020 season offered much optimism. The Big Red had back lefty Teat; righty attackman John Piatelli, a rugged Boston native, who scored forty-five goals the previous year; Canadian midfielder Brendan Donville (twenty goals, fourteen assists); sophomore defender Dom Doria; and standout goalkeeper Chayse Ierlan. The previous season was a letdown on many levels, and Coach Peter Milliman, assistants Connor Buczek and Jordan Stevens, and volunteer Paolo Ciferri were leaving nothing to chance. "Practices were battles," says Joe Bartolotto, a junior longstick midfielder. "If you weren't giving it your all, you got kicked out. If you half-assed anything the coaches would say, 'Get out, try again tomorrow.' It was intense." In one practice Milliman and his assistants kicked out four players in the first five minutes. "We were pushing those guys," Buczek says now, "harder than they'd ever been pushed before."

Cornell's 2020 season opener on the road against Albany on February 15 was played in subfreezing temperatures. To save money on accommodations, Cornell departed the morning of the game for the three-hour bus trip and came back in the evening. The bus left around 6 a.m., in pitch black, with temperatures around negative ten degrees. In the starting attack that day, alongside Piatelli and Teat, was freshman Mikey Long, from Mendham, New Jersey. Cornell won, 19–10. The Big Red kept rolling, beating Towson, Ohio State, and High Point, then entered a contest against second-ranked Penn State in early March, part of the Crown Lacrosse Classic in Charlotte, North Carolina. During practice that week, Cornell's face-off specialist and a longstick defender got into a full-blown fist fight. "The 2020 season, we felt pissed off and bitter," Bartolotto says. "At its core, we wanted to get back to how we do things. . . . No one owes you anything, nothing is guaranteed. Focus on the inputs, don't worry about the outputs. Control the controllables."

The matchup against Penn State was highly anticipated. The Nittany Lions featured redshirt senior Grant Ament, from Doylestown, Pennsylvania. As a sophomore at Haverford School in 2013, Ament was named MVP of the prestigious Inter-Ac tournament. As a senior in 2015, he set school single-season records with 120 points and 83 assists. His parents both graduated from Penn State, as did his twin brothers. Despite many suitors, Ament was interested in only one school. As a redshirt junior in 2019, Ament led the Nittany Lions to their first Championship Weekend. He finished the year with an NCAA record 96 assists, an average of 5.7 per game. That included nine assists in a regular season victory over Cornell and eight in an NCAA quarterfinal win over Loyola (Maryland). He was nearly as prolific in 2020. In five games entering the contest in Charlotte, Ament had eleven goals and twenty-three assists, nearly seven points per game. Cornell's coaches devised a defense specially for him. Called Fiji, it designated junior defender Gavin Adler to be left on an island—in lacrosse terms, no teammate would try to help Adler. Ament was Adler's assignment, and Cornell's chances relied heavily on his ability to keep the star in check. (It did not call for Adler to face-guard Ament, as had been done to Teat.)

Cornell flew to Charlotte on Saturday, March 7, for the Sunday game. The Crown Lacrosse Classic traditionally is held at American Legion Memorial Stadium, the site of a 1936 visit by President Franklin Delano Roosevelt, a couple USFL exhibitions in the 1980s, a 1996 Pearl Jam concert, and pro wrestling events featuring Ric Flair and Dusty Rhodes. In March 2020, the stadium's renovation project was behind schedule and not finished. The Cornell-Penn State game was moved to William Amos Hough High, in a northern Charlotte suburb.

With temperatures in the low sixties, a crowd of around four thousand people filled the aluminum bleachers to see a marquee matchup of teams ranked in the top seven. The setting did not necessarily befit the occasion. The banner outside the tiny press box called the venue "Where Huskies play tough," with snacks available at the "Hough Huskies Dawg Bites" concession stand. The vista included, at one end of the field, a row of white school buses. Cornell was assigned the modest visiting high school football locker room. At the end of the first quarter, Cornell led 8–2. By early in the third quarter, the Big Red led 13–5. The Nittany Lions responded. Early in the fourth quarter, the game was tied at 13. With around four minutes to play, Penn State took a 17–16 lead. With one minute to play, still trailing by a goal, Adler picked up a loose ball to give possession back to Cornell. After a mix-up on defense, Teat found himself guarded by a shortstick. His teammates, noting the mismatch, backed away. A one-on-one ensued. Teat moved back and forth, the defender doing well to follow every move. After at least ten seconds, the defender finally stumbled. Teat had his sliver of space and uncorked a lefty shot that eluded the goalkeeper. The game was tied with eighteen seconds left. On the ensuing face-off, Doria scooped a groundball from his knees, then spotted freshman face-off specialist Angelo Petrakis running wide open down the middle of the field. Still on one knee, Doria threw a pinpoint pass. Penn State, reluctant to leave Teat, Piatelli, or Long, let Petrakis shoot with eight seconds left. He buried it. Cornell won, 18–17.

In the tiny locker room that weeks earlier had hosted the Myers Park High Mustangs football team, the Big Red began its celebration, complete with its traditional victory song, the 1976 part-protest, part-underdog "Hurricane," by Bob Dylan. "Playing our song, jumping around, it's one of the best things ever," Doria says. Athletic trainer Jim Case, in his thirty-second year with the program, approached several players. "That's Cornell lacrosse," he told them, as recounted by Bartolotto. "That's the culture. That's the team I know and love." Teat finished with three goals, three assists, and two caused turnovers. Adler, too, largely kept Ament in check. Ament finished with six assists, though no goals, and two assists came on extra-man offense. "Everyone was so excited," Bartolotto says now. "We were all hugging and happy. And to hear what Jim Case said, that was confirmation. He knew George [Boiardi], he was ingrained in the culture of Cornell lacrosse. To get that validation from him meant we were doing the right things."

The lacrosse team's victory added fuel to the rapidly growing athletic excitement in Ithaca. The Cornell men's hockey team was ranked number one in the nation and earned a bye in the Eastern College Athletic Conference (ECAC) tournament. The conference playoffs were set to resume on March 13 in Ithaca. The women's hockey team also was ranked number one and was preparing for its NCAA tournament game against Mercyhurst in Ithaca on March 14. The lacrosse team flew back to Ithaca by way of Charlotte Douglas International Airport. Next up was its home opener, in six days, against Yale at Schoellkopf Field. The event was to be sandwiched between the hockey playoff games. On the TVs at the airport came reports that the BNP Paribas Open tennis tournament in California was canceled over concerns of the coronavirus pandemic. And amid a positive

COVID test, Marine Corps Base Quantico in Virginia began a Code Yellow alert. Its schools were closed until Wednesday to undergo an extensive cleaning.

On March 10, two days after the victory over Penn State, and amid scores of positive COVID-19 cases on college campuses across the country, Cornell announced in-person classes were set to be canceled. When students returned from spring break in early April, they would do so with virtual-only instruction. Professors were allowed to remain in their classrooms to teach for around two weeks before they, too, were to teach remotely. The vice president for student life called it "an extraordinary situation." The Cornell men's and women's hockey teams could continue their seasons, but spectators inside Lynah Rink were limited to one hundred. Cornell's lacrosse coaches and players called a meeting. "We all saw something was coming," Doria says now. "We thought, 'This might be it for the season.' There's nothing we can really do." Says Buczek, "We were all hoping it was a little overblown, and we'd continue playing. I don't think any of us envisioned what was going to happen next."

On March 11, citing the pandemic, and with an abundance of caution, the Ivy League canceled spring sports for the remainder of the season, along with canceling the rest of winter sports. "There was so much excitement for hockey and lacrosse," LaFalce says. "We had all these teams lined up to do amazing things. It was such a disappointment." Mike Levine, a standout attackman as a senior at Cornell in 1993, agreed. "There was this feeling we were always the bridesmaid and never the bride," he said. "We had Jeff Teat, we were 5–0, we were on the warpath to a championship." Milliman and the assistants urged the players to hang out together, to have as much time as possible, just in case the situation grew worse. Students had a nonstop party. The next seventy-two hours, Doria said, "were like the end of the world." The team also took time for one last informal gathering at Schoellkopf Field, their home turf, where they did not play a game in the 2020 season.

On March 13, the school suspended on-campus classes for three weeks. Then, on March 14, the lacrosse team received a text message far different from class schedules. Case, their beloved trainer who had been so enthused after the Penn State victory, had died unexpectedly from heart complications. He was fifty-five years old. Case was always available to listen to the players, who were sometimes homesick, sometimes lovesick, sometimes disappointed about playing time. He was known to lend a sympathetic ear, other times a more honest assessment. "Talk about devastating," Bartolotto says. "He was our dad away from home. If you were sick at 3 a.m. he'd be at your place. We all spent countless hours with him in the training room. . . . Every man on the roster needed him at some point, and he was always there. He wasn't just a trainer, he was also a mental health coach." Case was survived by his wife and three children. "He didn't share too much, and he didn't overstep unless you asked for it," Buczek says. "He was a great friend and mentor. And the timing of it made it that much harder. A lot of guys took that one pretty hard, especially as it was on the heels of everything that had happened, and the way things were going."

On March 20, the first positive COVID-19 cases hit Cornell's campus. Students, previously told to head to their permanent addresses by the end of the month, were now sent home. By this point the sports world was silent: The spring season was canceled for every school, not just the Ivies. Professional sports largely were canceled, or about to be so. In the final college lacrosse rankings, based on the truncated season in which every team had played around a half dozen games, the Big Red finished second, behind undefeated Syracuse.

On April 26, as Cornell lacrosse should have been preparing for senior day, the Ivy League tournament, and almost certainly the NCAA tournament, the players received a text message: Milliman was leaving to become head coach at Johns Hopkins. (An in-person notification was impossible, given that the entire student body had gone home. Not to mention the precautions in place banning large in-person gatherings. Milliman later told the Johns Hopkins alumni magazine he regretted not being able to meet the Cornell players in person.) Under Milliman, the Big Red went 28–10 in his two-plus seasons, and he was largely credited with recruiting Teat. "No one blamed him" for taking the Johns Hopkins job, Bartolotto said. Because of the pandemic, Milliman's three rounds of interviews at Johns Hopkins, according to a 2021 article in the alumni magazine, were entirely via Zoom, as was his introductory news conference.

The day after Milliman's departure, John Johnson II of Spectrum Sports broke the news that Buczek would be named interim coach, with Stevens staying on staff as defensive coordinator and associate head coach. Buczek was just twenty-six years old, Stevens roughly the same age. And the appointments were finally a bit of good news for a program badly in need of some. "I was telling anyone who would listen that the job has to go to Connor or Jordan," Bartolotto says. "Pete Milliman is a good guy and a good coach. We don't need to make any changes. With Connor and Jordan, we've got all we need. Don't bring anyone else in to run the ship." The students were home, Cornell's commencement ceremony took place online, and the future seemed very uncertain.

In the fall of the 2020–21 academic year, amid heavy coronavirus precautions, Cornell returned to campus, one of the few schools to do so. The athletes whose spring season had been canceled received a waiver from the NCAA, giving them an extra year of eligibility. It meant Teat was back. The Big Red also welcomed a strong freshman class, twelve players in total. They lived in three townhouses on the north side of campus, all in the same quad and within a few steps of each other.

For their first greetings on-campus, they and their parents were required to wear facial masks. Midfielder Hugh Kelleher and attackman CJ Kirst were roommates in the house with face-off specialist Mark Psyllos and attackman Monty Cook. In another townhouse, shortstick defender Kyle Smith and goalkeeper Walker Wallace were roommates, with defenders Caleb Newman and Jack Follows. The final townhouse featured attackman Andrew Dalton and defender Billy Kephart as roommates, with attackman Rory Graham and midfielder Ryan Sheehan. Amid the heightened coronavirus regulations, the freshmen were barred from visiting the upperclassmen for the first two weeks. Eventually, the freshmen were let out, four at a time, to visit the upperclassmen on a rotation.

Classes were almost entirely remote. The campus was "de-densified," meaning students who were in Ithaca were largely confined to their dorm rooms or areas immediately outside. When the school raised the threat level to yellow or above, masks or facial coverings were required, even outdoors. The first day back on campus, it went to yellow. Students, faculty, and staff were subject to random coronavirus testing; one report says the school tested twenty thousand people each week. A positive test meant quarantine for the person for several days. They would receive meals through delivery to their door. At times, visitors were barred from campus. "We pretty much were locked in those townhouses," Sheehan says now. "We were either going to be best friends in the first week or kill each other." Says Dalton, "There was nothing to do but sit in the townhouses and get to know each other." Players recall online classes, homework, playing lots of card games, and watching movies. The Ivy League canceled fall sports, though other conferences permitted them, albeit with heavy restrictions on who could attend the games (usually limited to students, faculty, staff, and parents of players).

Amid the cancellations, the lacrosse program was able to conduct a semblance of its off-season workouts. Sessions were limited to one hour and ten people. Attendees had to social distance—that is, not be within six feet of one another. To help, staff painted small boxes on the ground; players were asked to remain within the lines. The restrictions meant there was no chance to do offense against defense drills. One group of workouts took place in a makeshift weight room on the concourse level of the Crescent stands at Schoellkopf Field. The training staff brought a limited variety of weights—dumbbells, kettle bells, and resistance bands—to the area near the concession stands and bathrooms. Other workout areas appeared in the Crescent parking lot and the Ramin Room, an indoor turf field usually reserved for drills and scrimmages. One player recalled a brief weight-lifting area in the Cornell Athletic Hall of Fame. During the workouts, players were required to wear facial masks. Sheehan said at least once during heavy conditioning, he became sick to his stomach and vomited into a nearby trash can, only to immediately be asked to return to his box and put his facial covering back on.

Another anomaly: Because of the smaller number of participants, far more conditioning and skill sessions were needed to accommodate team members. Players often had one conditioning workout at 6 a.m. and a skills session at 7 p.m. It led to long days and unfamiliar times. "The coaches were pretty strict" about the COVID restrictions, Doria says. "Some of the fraternities and sports teams got in trouble for not following as closely. We didn't want to stick out in a bad way. But it was tough, the social aspect. That's an intangible force, or driver, for our team to get to know each other."

Whether the work would lead to anything concrete remained to be seen. In previous years, Cornell had met Maryland in a fall scrimmage, alternating locations between College Park, Maryland, and Ithaca. In the fall of 2020, the scrimmage was canceled. On November 12, the Ivy League canceled the upcoming 2020–21 winter sports season. (Most other leagues, at least for men's and women's basketball, decided to play.) The news threw Cornell's spring sports into jeopardy.

The Cornell freshman class that arrived during the COVID pandemic had one other distinction: They were the final class subject to the lacrosse phenomenon known as "early recruiting." It began in December 2009. Spencer Parks, a sophomore attackman-midfielder at St. Paul's (Maryland) outside Baltimore, and coming off a strong summer with the Baltimore Crabs club team, committed to the University of North Carolina. Geoff Shannon in *Inside Lacrosse* reported Parks was the first known high school sophomore to make public his college commitment. The following year, goalkeeper Ryan Feit, a sophomore at Syosset (New York) High, committed to Johns Hopkins. In the summer of 2012 came the previously unthinkable. Ryan Conrad of Loyola-Blakefield (Maryland), following his freshman year of high school, committed to play for the University of Virginia. *The Baltimore Sun* reported that at the time Conrad committed, he was fifteen years old. Weeks after Conrad's commitment, Forry Smith of Haverford (Pennsylvania) School committed to Johns Hopkins before finishing his first semester of high school. "Spencer Parks was the catalyst," says Ty Xanders, national recruiting expert for Prep Lacrosse who covered the early recruiting phenomenon for *Inside Lacrosse*. "From there, the floodgates opened up. Kids were committing earlier and earlier. Coaches were thinking, well, if everyone else is doing it, I better be, too. It really created a frenzy. At that point, the toothpaste was out of the tube."

In October 2012, US Lacrosse, the governing body for the sport in the United States, issued a position statement. It raised concerns over the push to a year-round recruiting calendar and urged men's and women's college coaches to "exert their considerable influence to lead reform of the NCAA recruiting calendar, limit the age at which student-athletes begin the recruiting process, and agree not to attend or participate in recruiting events that infringe on the academic calendar of student-athletes." The head of US Lacrosse went one step further. "No 14-year old is positioned to make a wise choice on where to get a college education," Steve Stenersen told *The Sun*. His last statement sounded the alarm. "Right now," he told *The Sun*, "it's the Wild West out there."

Stenersen was from Baltimore and played in the 1970s in the private school league, the Maryland Interscholastic Athletic Association, which boasted some of the country's best lacrosse. He later starred on North Carolina's 1981 and 1982 NCAA title teams. He was hardly an outsider. Yet his words had little to no impact. More high school freshmen committed to college. Eventually, a handful of players selected their college while in eighth grade. As Xanders notes, the widespread practice of recruiting fourteen-year-olds gave lacrosse a black eye. "Rising high school freshmen . . . are being offered [scholarships or roster spots] by ACC schools and the 'who's who' of lacrosse, and they are being pressured to make a decision," he says. "Coaches were looking at kids who were 5-foot-8, 140 pounds, and trying to see what they'd develop into in the next four-to-eight years. Asking questions like, 'How tall are your parents? How tall is your grandfather?' It was a landscape that rewarded kids who were a little older [as freshmen] and who developed quicker." The Ivy League fell prey to early recruiting, with a codicil. It required high schoolers to say they had committed "to the admissions process" at their school. Still, Xanders says at least one or two Ivy schools were essentially accepting lacrosse recruits based on three semesters of high school transcripts. "It was not a good time for lacrosse," Xanders says now. "I think it must've been hard for some of the coaches to look at themselves in the mirror. To say, 'I'm doing the best for my program,' or 'I'm doing the best for lacrosse,' there wasn't any of that. It was a rat race. And once you were in it, you were in it."

In the spring of 2017, sensing the issue had become uncontrollable, the men's and women's coaches associations requested the NCAA adopt lacrosse-only legislation that would ban contact between college coaches and a high school player until September 1 of the player's junior year. In mid-April 2017, to the surprise of many, the NCAA adopted the measure. To the further surprise of many, it took effect immediately. (The rule offers earlier contact for the service academies and some Division III programs, which have longer admissions processes.) "It was really driven by the women's coaches," Xanders says. "We have to thank them, they were the drivers of the change. . . . I was in shock when the NCAA passed it. I was told, repeatedly, the NCAA doesn't want a bigger rule book. Also people were skeptical the NCAA would do a lacrosse-only rule." Xanders notes the only downside was for players who had already committed as eighth graders or freshmen in high school in 2017. Suddenly, with the new rule effective immediately, they were banned from having contact with the coaches to whom they had committed.

One of those players was Ryan Sheehan, a midfielder from outside Syracuse, New York. His lacrosse career began with a lie. At the age of four, his parents fudged his paperwork and signed him up for a summer lacrosse camp meant for children ages five and up. It helped that the camp was hosted by LeMoyne University near the family home. It helped further that Sheehan's dad was LeMoyne's coach. "That was the first time I put on a lacrosse helmet," Ryan Sheehan says now. "I've barely taken it off since." The younger Sheehan progressed to the point that, for the 2017 season, he was set to be a rare freshman to earn playing time at nationally recognized West Genesee (New York) High. Colleges took note, especially Jeff Tambroni at Penn State, a West Genesee alum. The Nittany Lions began recruiting Sheehan, inviting him to a home football game against Temple in mid-September 2016, Sheehan's freshman year. More than one hundred thousand fans filled the immense Beaver Stadium, taking part in a "stripe-out," where seating sections alternated wearing blue or white, the school colors. Sheehan watched warmups from the field as future NFL players Saquon Barkley, Chris Godwin, and Trace McSorley prepared to lead the Nittany Lions to a 34–27 victory. Soon after, Sheehan accepted the offer from Penn State. He was fourteen years old.

Then came the NCAA rule change, in the spring of Sheehan's freshman year. Because it took effect immediately, Sheehan essentially went eighteen months with almost no interaction with Tambroni and his assistants. In his junior year at West Genesee, Sheehan took another official visit to Penn State, again for a football game, again part of the "stripe-out." The Nittany Lions defeated Iowa, 30–24. Sheehan says it was unforgettable being so close to major college football, within feet of future NFL stars, with more than one hundred thousand people filling a stadium set for deafening noise for the next three hours. A wide, if unspoken, rule stated that college coaches considered the players who committed in their freshman year of high school, prior to the NCAA intervention, recruitable. Sheehan fielded calls from other programs. He accepted a visit to Cornell, much closer to his home and a school at which his father could attend any games that did not conflict with LeMoyne's schedule.

On his trip to Ithaca, Sheehan wound up in the apartment of junior Griffin Buczek, younger brother of Connor, and his roommates, all of whom were on the lacrosse team. The visit featured none of the trappings of Big Ten football. Still, Sheehan felt a strong connection. "Those guys were obviously so close," Sheehan says. "They sat there talking to each other about Cornell culture and holding each other accountable. But they also busted each other's chops and had fun. It sounds corny, but that culture was really where I saw myself. The hard hat, all of it." Entering the spring of 2020, his senior year, Sheehan flipped to Cornell. It was one of the few highlights of his spring. There was no season because of the pandemic, no senior banquet until August, when Central New York showed signs of improvement. "It was a weird time," Sheehan says. "I try not to think about it."

As Sheehan and the rest of the Cornell students left Ithaca after the fall semester, they joined everyone else in hoping the worst of COVID-19 was done. "We finally made it," Bartolotto says. "That [2020 fall semester] was the toughest fall in my life. By a mile." In late November, right around Thanksgiving, the Ivy League said spring sports would not start until March 1 at the earliest. Still, Ivy League President Robin Harris told *Inside Lacrosse* that administrators were doing everything they could. "We're anxious to get back and compete," she said. "Everyone recognizes they've already lost a season. There's not a single person who wants to see [spring sport athletes] lose another season. We are committed to returning when it's safe to do so."

3

IT'S GREAT TO BE HERE

Cornell's 2021 spring semester, with the pandemic still visible, featured several changes to the academic calendar. Gone was spring break. It was replaced by two sets of "wellness days," one in mid-March, the other in late April. Classes were offered in person, online, and as a "hybrid." For lacrosse, in mid-January, the Ivy League updated its guidance from Thanksgiving, saying there was no timetable for games. Back in Ithaca was attackman Jeff Teat, first-team all-American in 2018, second-team pick in 2019. The son of a longtime professional indoor lacrosse player, Teat was the number-one selection in the September 2020 supplemental draft of the National Lacrosse League, a professional indoor venture. Teat could have left Cornell after the 2020 season to play in the indoor league and then moved on to the nascent Premier Lacrosse League, a professional outdoor league. He also could have transferred to a school far more likely to field a team in 2021, as did standouts at other Ivy League schools. "He could have been playing elsewhere," assistant coach Jordan Stevens says of Teat. "He wanted to come back and try to win a national title at Cornell. He said, 'If I'm going to play in college, it's only going to be for Cornell.'" Teat's return meant the Big Red had back just about every main contributor from the undefeated 2020 squad that showed so much promise. The coaches tinkered with having lefty Teat on attack and highly regarded freshman CJ Kirst, also a lefty, running out of the box as a midfielder with Canadian standout Jonathan Donville.

Around most of men's Division I lacrosse, the mood for 2021 was cautiously optimistic. An informal poll sent to coaches in the late fall by *Inside Lacrosse* said 87 percent had a moderate to high expectation there would be a season. Zero

CHAPTER 3

percent thought it would be canceled again. This was in part because college football and men's and women's college basketball completed their seasons. Amid waiting for news from the Ivy League, dominoes started to fall, in the wrong direction for the athletes. In early February, *Inside Lacrosse* reported Yale would not field a team. Around forty players had decided not to enroll for the spring semester, thus saving a year of eligibility should the season be canceled again. The move reflected a growing unease among the league's spring sports athletes and supporters. Yale senior Cal Christofori, baseball team captain and starting catcher, wrote an open letter to the Ivy League Presidents Council that he also posted on social media. "I am writing to you . . . to emphasize and reinforce the importance of having a spring sports season this year," he wrote. "We have seen effective COVID-19 health and safety protocols be implemented across a range of intercollegiate sports already, and are confident they can be more than upheld in the Ivy League this spring. Furthermore, with student-athletes having the ability to forego the season and retain eligibility, they are free to make decisions regarding individual health and safety independently."

The Wall Street Journal reported in its February 15 editions that Alibaba cofounder Joe Tsai, a letter winner in lacrosse at Yale in the 1980s, offered to build a sequestered "bubble" at his own expense—at the cost of several million dollars—to host a three-week, single-site Ivy League men's and women's lacrosse season. (Ivy League presidents, the *Journal* reported, rebuffed the idea.) Another Ivy League alum, former Brown football player Mark Warden, and his wife, a former Yale women's hockey player, wrote a letter that made the rounds among athletes and parents. "If anything, the Ivy League should be on the forefront of developing ways for student activities, including athletics, to reopen as opposed to having their actions suggest that there is a problem and they don't have a solution," Warden wrote. "They certainly have the experts and money to make it happen."

Three days after the *Wall Street Journal* article, and as much of the rest of lacrosse prepared for its season openers, the Ivy League Council of Presidents announced its decision. There would be no spring sports. Practices were permitted, and the group did not rule out limited nonleague competition if health and other conditions improved. "These are the necessary decisions for the Ivy League," read the statement, "in the face of the health concerns posed by the ongoing and dangerous pandemic."

Around three-dozen lacrosse Cornell players, again to preserve a season of eligibility, withdrew from classes, with no guarantee of returning. "There was concern there was going to be an exodus of Cornell's really good players," says Tom LaFalce. Two days after the cancellation, Cornell announced a one-time exemption: Spring athletes would be able to compete in 2022, even if they did so as full-time graduate students, something previously barred by league rules. "We were like, 'What the heck? We already took off,'" says Dom Doria, a starting defenseman. Doria was enrolled in industrial and labor relations and says without his counselor's hard work to find classes that could keep him on track to graduate, he might have had to forgo his final season of eligibility. Bartolotto, too, withdrew from school, targeting the 2022 season. "Taking a 'leave of absence' from school, in order to play another year, I was like yeah, I'll climb Mount Everest to play one more year," Bartolotto says. "But we were pushing our lives off for another year, too. In the moment there was anger and resentment." Doria, Bartolotto, and midfielder Matt Licciardi left Ithaca and took a long road trip down the East Coast, where COVID precautions were less strict.

Teat decided against coming back. He used the spring of 2021 to prepare for the upcoming NLL season and graduate. Donville, too, entered the transfer portal, eyeing the masters in journalism program at the University of Maryland, a program not offered at Cornell. A handful of other players, for various reasons, some financial, others because they already had a job lined up, declined to use the waiver and planned to graduate and take part in the virtual graduation ceremony in late May. As conditions improved, a few Ivy League teams played a single game or two games that spring. The Big Red, with twenty players, was unable to schedule such contests. "We knew there was no light at the end of the tunnel," Stevens says. "We hoped the practices would just keep the standard alive." The only goalkeeper was Parker Henderer, a senior from Gulph Mills, Pennsylvania, a three-year reserve. Henderer had grown up playing baseball, the sport his father played at Division III Trinity College (Connecticut) before graduating from Johns Hopkins Medical School and becoming the chair of ophthalmology at Temple University School of Medicine. Parker Henderer switched to lacrosse in middle school and never played a position other than goalkeeper. His father, a highly respected eye surgeon and professor, spent hours shooting on his son in the backyard.

In the spring of 2021 in Ithaca, Henderer now faced shots from Teat, one of the best in the world. As the only goalkeeper, Henderer was set to see a lot of shots. To offset the dearth of players, Buczek, Stevens, and assistant Paolo Ciferri, a letter winner at Syracuse, often suited up for practice. "More than anything else," Buczek says, "it was an outlet, a way for the guys to put on pads and compete. Parker was amazing as the singular goalie. He was the guy who allowed us to keep playing." Otherwise, the standard did not change, even without games. Stevens said the goal of spring 2021 was not so much to improve. "We were just trying to give the guys, especially the seniors, an experience that was fun," he says. "Life around then was miserable. We knew what college life was, we knew what Cornell lacrosse was, and this wasn't it. Those guys were tough as nails. They held onto the standard."

The 2021 college lacrosse season—without the Ivy League—finished on Memorial Day in East Hartford, Connecticut. In the championship, Virginia led Maryland by a goal with ten seconds remaining. Maryland freshman Luke Wierman won a face-off and raced toward the goal. As the Cavaliers locked off Maryland's attackmen, it was obvious the game came down to Wierman against Virginia goalkeeper Alex Rode. Wierman shot; Rode made the save, then ran out the clock in a 17–16 victory. The lasting image afterward was an inconsolable Wierman being comforted by his teammates and Coach John Tillman.

In the fall of the 2021–22 academic year, students returned to Cornell still navigating coronavirus precautions. Because of the cancellations and eligibility waivers, the Big Red lacrosse program essentially had two freshman classes, two groups whose eligibility would end in 2025. The jewels of the classes were roommates Kirst and Hugh Kelleher. Kirst's initial recruitment predated the NCAA September 1 rule. The Johns Hopkins coaches hosted Kirst as an eighth grader and his mother for an on-campus visit. When the NCAA moved all recruiting to the start of junior year, the recruitment slowed. As a sophomore at Delbarton (New Jersey) School in 2018, Kirst scored thirty-one goals and added eight assists; the Green Wave won the New Jersey state tournament of champions and finished ranked number two in the nation. As a junior he showed even more promise. Kirst scored sixty goals and added thirty assists, and the Green Wave finished twelfth in the nation. By this time Kirst was drawing attention from any number of schools, including in the Big East and Big Ten, which offer athletic scholarships. Kirst's three older brothers played Division I lacrosse, and a younger brother showed promise as a high school goalie; their late father had been a starting goalie at Rutgers. Peter Milliman and his assistants threw Cornell's hat in the ring. "I remember having such a strong connection with his mother and his family," Stevens says. "What he wanted, we had. And what we needed, he was excellent at." *Inside Lacrosse* ranked Kirst as the number nine incoming freshman, placing him on par with Max Seibald, *IL*'s number five incoming freshman in 2005; Rob Pannell, the number one incoming postgrad student in 2008; and Teat, number one incoming freshman in 2016. At 6-feet-1, 190 pounds, Kirst would take over the starting lefty attack spot vacated by Teat.

Kelleher was a lacrosse-football standout at Douglas MacArthur High in Wantagh, New York. In the summer of 2018, Kelleher was entering his junior year of high school when then-assistant Buczek watched him play in a summer tournament in Philadelphia. Kelleher was 6-feet-2, 205 pounds, the son of a retired NYPD detective, and showed Buczek both good and bad. "It was a super hot day, and I was never good in hot weather," Kelleher says. "I'd go out and score a goal, then throw up, then go out again, come back and throw up." He was invited to

Cornell for an on-campus visit. By mistake, his father signed Kelleher up instead for prospect day, where coaches evaluate those who are interested in Cornell, not as much the other way around. "I wasn't supposed to play on my visit," Kelleher says. "But I think it helped me out. I guess I did well." Milliman expressed an interest. The next day, Kelleher committed. By then, his junior season of football was underway. Kelleher was single-handedly winning games. Against Elmont (New York) in early November 2018, he rushed for 190 yards and scored the game's only touchdown after scooping a blocked punt and racing to the end zone in a 7–0 victory. He finished the season with 1,221 rushing yards and 12 touchdowns while also starting as a linebacker and leading the Generals to the playoffs.

Kelleher's mother pushed him to attend an Ivy League school, hence the attraction of Cornell. Then Penn football entered the picture. "It was a pretty tough decision to make," Kelleher says. Around the time of Penn's football interest, late fall 2018, Stevens arrived for his prearranged home visit. He essentially re-recruited Kelleher on the spot. "Coach Stevens's home visit came at a good time," Kelleher says. "After that visit, there was no way I could de-commit." Fate intervened, too. In late January 2019, Kelleher was in attendance when his club coach was inducted into the Long Island Metro Lacrosse Hall of Fame. Also in attendance that night was Richie Moran. The two were introduced. A couple nights later, Kelleher took the court for the MacArthur basketball team in a road game against Mepham (New York). In attendance again was Moran, watching the future Cornell lacrosse player. "He came to watch the whole game," Kelleher says. "He remembered what we had talked about, that I was at MacArthur and also played basketball. . . . I always thought that would be the best skill to have, to remember everything. He definitely had it." As a senior in 2019, Kelleher enjoyed an even better football season: 1,849 yards rushing and 21 touchdowns, adding 83 tackles as a linebacker. He won the inaugural Tom Flatley Award as the top football-lacrosse player in Nassau County. Still, he did not budge from his Cornell commitment. By the fall of 2021, he'd grown to 6-feet-2, 220 pounds, and in Cornell's rigorous off-season strength testing, he produced one of the top marks, 315 pounds in the bench press. Kelleher was penciled into a spot on the starting midfield, a hard-dodging right-hander who could initiate the 1-3-2 offense, force an immediate double-team, and get the defense moving.

A couple weeks after 2021–22 classes began, the rest of the freshmen received their formal introduction to Moran. September 11 is the anniversary of the terror attacks in New York and Washington, DC. Eamon McEneaney, who led Cornell to the 1976 and 1977 NCAA titles, was killed in the Twin Towers. He was forty-six years old, a husband, a father of four, a star attackman, and a prolific writer and poet (a book of his poems was published posthumously by Cornell University Library). Every year on the anniversary of his death, the team would gather to listen to Moran's stories about McEneaney, about family, and about Cornell lacrosse. The setting on September 11, 2021, was the three bronze plaques on the brown brick wall facing Schoellkopf Field, near the entrance and exit the team uses to take the field. (The plaques were for McEneaney, George Boiardi, and Jay Gallagher, team captain in 1974, who died of cancer at the age of forty.)

Moran was eighty-four years old, and his health was rapidly in decline due to pulmonary fibrosis, kidney issues, and dialysis. He was losing weight and needed a walker to get around. Steve Lawrence, a longtime friend of Moran and coauthor of a book with him, was with Moran for his 9/11 visit. The team went straight from a workout to listen to the legendary coach. "With the plaque honoring Eamon in the background," Lawrence later wrote in the *Ithaca Times*, "the beloved coach gave what everyone knew would be his last speech to the team.... [Players] were sweaty, hungry, worn out from a tough workout, but they sat there attentively, leaning in to hear what Richie was trying to say. His voice was faint and faltering, but this group ... who likely never knew just how much this tradition meant to Richie, grasped the power of the moment." After Moran's remarks, as a tradition, each freshman introduced himself. Even in his frail health, Moran recognized Kelleher and remembered having seen him play high school basketball. "He already knew our names and position and hometown," says Danny Caddigan, a freshman attackman. "I'll never forget it. People said he was a great connector of generations. I saw it there." During his remarks, the seniors crowded closest to Moran, to hear him better. Freshmen like Sheehan were toward the back. Because everyone listened so intently, so quietly, he was able to hear most of Moran's message. One part that stuck with him: "Coach Moran said, 'These are your brothers. Love them like your brothers, whether you want to punch them in the face or give them a hug.'"

As the fall progressed, and campuses across the country largely reemerged from the pandemic, it became obvious the Ivy League would have a lacrosse season. To prepare, Cornell's fall workouts included weekly full-field scrimmages. "We were fired up," Doria says. "We were ready to go." Mikey Long agreed. "There was so much pent-up energy," he says. "The Ivy programs were hit very hard." After losing nearly two full seasons of lacrosse, Doria says even the cold-weather, 6:15 a.m. practices were welcome. After a few weeks, Buczek says, the players who had romanticized returning to play lacrosse remembered it was also very hard work. Here, the seniors stepped in. "So much of lacrosse is mental," Doria says. "Probably 90 percent of it is mental. You can get bogged down in all the pressure of lacrosse and classes and trying to balance it all with extra film study and extra time on the field. You can't lose sight of being loose and playing loose. I was trying to be enthusiastic. It's easy to be grumpy when it's freezing cold during a morning practice. But yelling, hooting, and hollering can be infectious. It can get the team going."

When that didn't work, Doria and Bartolotto devised another trick: They would get into a fight with each other. "That got the boys going," Doria says. "They started yelling and screaming and got everyone pumped up. Later, Coach Stevens said, 'Was that fight really necessary? Did that make our team better?' And we looked at each other and said yeah, we think it did."

There was a fall scrimmage, and the countdown began to the main intrasquad scrimmage on February 1 and the season opener against Albany roughly two weeks later. "We missed lacrosse," Kelleher says now. "We missed the contact, we missed everything." Added Bartolotto, "We needed guys to be bought in right away. Because we had all seen how quickly this can be taken away." The annual fall scrimmage against Maryland took place at Delbarton School in New Jersey. An official score was not kept, but Kirst entered in the second quarter and, according to one eyewitness account, scored at least four goals. After the scrimmage, in the handshake line, Cornell director of player development Mark Wittink greeted star midfielder Jonathan Donville, once of Cornell, now in grad school at Maryland. Donville hugged Wittink, smiled, and said of facing his former team and close friends, "That was fun. Let's never do it again."

Autumn workouts at Cornell are a little different from most Division I programs. Per Ivy League rules, the fall is limited to twelve hours on-field. (The NCAA permits twenty hours of off-season work, which is used by most Division I programs.) This is also a time for the freshmen to learn more about the expectations of playing lacrosse at Cornell. For weight lifting and conditioning, players were expected to wear their gray T-shirts with red "Cornell Lacrosse" written on the left chest. The shirts are called a Teagle, named for Teagle Hall, the gray brick, Collegiate Gothic style building near Schoellkopf Field where athletes are given their equipment. The Teagle is to be worn tucked into red shorts or black shorts, depending on the day. During drills, players are expected to run from one spot to the next, not walk nor amble, all amid a drumbeat of encouragement and cajoling. Cornell may be hampered by having eight fewer fall practice sessions than other Division I programs. It compensates with additional conditioning.

Here, center stage belongs to Tom Howley, the team's strength and conditioning coach. A native of Youngstown, Ohio, in the late 1980s he played offensive line at Tulane. His position coach encouraged him to give strength and conditioning a try. Howley arrived at Cornell in July 1995 from East Carolina University, having worked with its football, basketball, and baseball teams. He had never seen a lacrosse game in person, only on television. On his first day on Cornell's campus he went from his office in Teagle Hall across the street to Schoellkopf Field and the coaches' offices. It was summer, and the only door that was open was that of the lacrosse office and then-head coach Moran. Howley walked in and introduced himself. The two spoke for several minutes. Howley, seeing no other coaches present, went back to his office. Within a few minutes, his phone rang. On the other line was a man with a heavy Scottish accent, asking rapid-fire questions. "And I thought, who is this? No one even knows I'm here," Howley says now. "There's literally no one on campus." After about a minute the Scottish accent disappeared, replaced by a shrill finger-whistle and "Big Boy!" This gave it away. "I was a victim of one of Coach Moran's pranks on my first day," Howley says. "That began my relationship with the sport of lacrosse."

The main intrasquad scrimmage arrived on February 1, the first day full practices are allowed in the Ivy League. (Other Division I teams start a couple weeks earlier.) It was played in Schoellkopf Field, with temperatures in the mid-thirties. The scrimmage pits the starters and fourth string against the second and third strings. Goalkeeper Wyatt Knust, a freshman from Tampa, Florida, noted he was on the same team as senior Chayse Ierlan, the starting goalie. "That basically means I'm fourth string," Knust says. "I figured during the scrimmage I'd get to play the second half." Halftime arrived. The coaches told Ierlan to prepare to stay on the field. At the start of the fourth quarter, they asked Ierlan keep playing. Of the forty-eight players on the roster, Knust was the only one who didn't get into the scrimmage. "In the moment, that was tough," he says.

Knust had begun playing the sport in Florida through his father, an attackman-midfielder at Gettysburg (Pennsylvania), a strong Division III program. Initially Knust, too, played offense. At age ten he was the lefty attackman for the B team, or lower-level team, for his club in Florida. The team's goalie was ill suited for the position given his penchant to turn his back on hard shots from the outside. "As the season progressed he got more and more scared of the ball," Knust says. "It was pretty frustrating from my point of view. My dad was the coach, and at halftime of one game I told him, maybe somebody else should go in goal. And he said, 'You can't say that unless you're willing to do it.'" With that, Knust put on the goalie's protective pads, picked up a goalie's stick, and went onto the field. He found he liked the position, so much so he stuck with it. He progressed to the point that by his junior year at H. B. Plant High in a Tampa suburb, in the fall of 2019, he was being recruited by Patriot League and Ivy League schools. He went on a few recruiting trips; nothing panned out. Then the pandemic hit in March 2020, and Knust suddenly had no path to play in college and no games upcoming in which to try to impress someone.

A few teams from the New England Small College Athletic Conference (NESCAC) in Division III reached out. And that is where he may have landed if not for one of his club coaches, Todd Francis, a member of the 1987 Cornell NCAA runner-up squad. Cornell's recruited goalie in Knust's class suddenly switched to Notre Dame. That left an opening. Francis called the Cornell coaches. They watched Knust's film and liked what they saw; they also noted that Knust was an excellent student. Cornell's campus was closed to visitors, so there was no chance for Knust to visit. He also had heard that Buczek liked to shoot on goalie recruits before offering them a spot. That, too, could not happen, given the distance from Ithaca to Tampa. Still, the Big Red needed a goalie, and Buczek waived his shooting-on-recruits preference and offered Knust a place on the team. "I never visited the campus," Knust says. "I never even met the coaches in person. I just committed on the spot." Now he was meeting with the goalie coach, Ciferri, asking just how far down the depth chart he was. "He said, 'That was bad coaching more than anything you did, not to get you at least a couple minutes,'" Knust says now. "That really motivated me to start focusing. I didn't want to be buried on the bottom. I wanted to show them I belonged." Within days, Walker Wallace, the goalie recruit in the class above Knust but still a freshman eligibility-wise, was injured in practice. Knust moved up the depth chart.

Another newcomer found practice even more trying. Bartolotto and Doria recognized Kelleher's immense talent and his likely spot in the starting midfield. They also surmised he would be the target of opponents. So during drills, offense against defense, they acted the role of older brothers. This was especially apparent in a drill called Pressure Triangles, shortened to Pressure T's. The object was for an offensive player to catch a pass, then throw it successfully to a teammate, all while being hounded by a defender. To exit the drill, the player had to catch and then complete his pass without a drop. Otherwise, he remained on the field. It was constant motion, a blur, with no time limit; it could last three minutes or fifteen. To this, Bartolotto and Doria added a twist. They impeded Kelleher, even illegally, with jersey pulling, grabbing his stick to make sure his pass was errant or dropped, even an elbow to the back or ribs. Moreover, each time Kelleher was in line, Bartolotto or Doria made sure to be the one to go against him, sometimes even tossing a teammate to the side if Kelleher skipped ahead. "We wanted him to be ready," Bartolotto says now. "In a game, if someone cheap shots you, are you going to stop and complain or keep going and hope the ref sees it?" With the constant attention, Kelleher struggled to do the catch-one, complete-one. He was in the drill for ten minutes at a time. "I've never been so tired," Kelleher says. "Sometimes the drill ended and I would look down and the field was changing colors." In the instances when Stevens wanted to prove a point, he would keep Pressure T's going even longer than usual. To this, Doria and Bartolotto interjected one of their fights, just to stop action for a few seconds to give everyone else a breather. Eventually, Stevens caught on. "That's great you guys are fighting," he said, "but when you're done you still have to complete a pass." (Says Stevens, "Rules are rules.")

"Joe was our archnemesis on the field," Kelleher says. "But he was also my biggest role model. He pushed me to the limit. He was trying to make us better with every single rep. They'd call Pressure T's and we'd say oh shit, it's time to battle." Doria, a six-feet-four defender and four-year starter, targeted Kirst. While the action was on the other side of the field, and away from the vision of the coaches, Doria would roll down Kirst's socks or take the top of his stick and rub Kirst's elbow pads up and down. "Joe and I took pride in being a little cheap," Doria says. "It was like, 'Are you going to bitch on gameday if someone does that to you?' Those are the little nuances." Fifth-year senior John Piatelli, too, took Kelleher and Kirst under his wing, the good cop to Doria and Bartolotto's bad cops. The righty attackman, with a hard outside shot and good hands to catch inside passes, indefatigable in hounding the opposing team while trying to clear the ball from defense to offense, would take Kirst and Kelleher for nightly passing and shooting practice on the goals at Schoellkopf Field. Once, deep into a late-winter evening, the trio, three of Cornell's starting six on offense, were passing and shooting as a light snow fell around them. Kelleher later likened it to being in a snow globe.

Finally, after 713 days, Cornell took the field for a regular season game, the 2022 season opener on February 19 against Albany at Schoellkopf Field. The rest of the sport barely noticed. In the Inside Lacrosse/KANE preseason media poll, no Ivy League team was ranked in the top five; only Yale was in the top ten; Cornell found itself at number fifteen. (Virginia and Maryland, who played for the championship the previous year, were ranked numbers one and two.) The temperature for the opener was twenty-five degrees, and even though it was sunny, the referees wore heavy black winter jackets that obscured their black-and-white pinstripes. Cornell's starting attack was lefty Kirst, Piatelli at the righty spot, and sophomore Mikey Long as the quarterback. The midfield featured Kelleher, with seniors Aiden Blake and Matt Licciardi. The starting defense was Doria, senior Ian Jacobs, and junior Gavin Adler, with Ierlan in goal.

Junior Angelo Petrakis, the hero of the Penn State game in March 2020, won the opening face-off. Less than ninety seconds into the game Cornell scored, Piatelli firing a low-angle shot from the right wing past the goalie. Petrakis won the ensuing face-off, and Cornell scored again, this time on a close shot by Kirst—the first goal of his career, assisted by reserve JJ Lombardi. More goals followed, from Kirst, Kelleher, and senior Billy Coyle, a reserve attackman-midfielder. On its first six possessions, Cornell scored five goals and coasted to a 16–8 victory. Other freshmen joined Kirst and Kelleher in the lineup. Chris Davis, a shortstick defender from Essex Junction, Vermont, finished the opener with a team-high five groundballs. Caddigan, a righty shooter from Long Island, made the extra-man offense and scored a goal in the second game of the year, a 9–5 victory over Lehigh in Bethlehem, Pennsylvania. The third game was an unimpressive

14–10 victory over visiting Hobart. Afterward, the seniors cleared the air. "No one else has been through what we have," they told the team. "No one else lost their trainer, then lost their head coach to another school, then lost a season. And you don't think you're tougher than the team in the other locker room?"

The Big Red had won nine of its first ten games before entering the highly anticipated showdown with Syracuse in the Carrier Dome. The venue offers a unique experience in lacrosse; before the home team takes the field, the stadium lights are turned off, followed by deafening music and a mini light show. At the end of the first quarter, the Orange led 7–2, and Ierlan had yet to make a save. On the sideline, the coaches rolled the dice. Knust had moved up to second on the depth chart. At the start of the second quarter in Syracuse, Knust replaced Ierlan. "It's just another day in practice," Doria told him, "except we have people watching us." Adler was more succinct. He gave the freshman a fist bump and said, "We're going to win this game." Says Knust, "I nodded my head and said, yes we are. That was it."

At halftime, the Orange led 11–6, and Knust had made a couple saves. The coaches stuck with him. The game was in overtime and tied at 15 when Kelleher scored the winner. Piatelli finished with six goals, and Knust made eight saves, giving up eight goals. "What I remember most," Kelleher says, "was how cool John Piatelli was during the game. Even when he made a turnover, and you knew he was furious inside, there was no stress on his face. It was always, 'We're going to be fine. Let's go make the next play.'"

Next came the Army visit to Schoellkopf Field on April 16. The night before the game, an Army player called Moran's house and asked which team he'd be rooting for. It wasn't a prank call like the ones for which the legendary coach was known. The caller was Ryan Spostio, a junior reserve midfielder for Army and Moran's grandson. According to Kevin Brown of *Inside Lacrosse*, Moran replied, in his raspy voice, "Ryan, blood runs thicker than water." By this point Moran, around two years into near-daily hours-long dialysis, was in a major struggle with his health. He somehow made it to Schoellkopf Field with Lawrence and sat in his usual spot on the side opposite the Crescent stands, one floor above the press box, accessible through an elevator. Early in the third quarter, Sposito, recently promoted from the scout team, scored a goal. It was his first of the year. Midway through the third quarter he scored again. Around two minutes later he scored his third goal. Army won, 17–10; Sposito's three goals were a team high. The following day, Easter Sunday, Moran's family gathered, with Lawrence joining. Moran decided to stop dialysis. The end was near. He held on for a few more days, though he did not attend the home finale against Brown on April 23, a 13–8 loss in which Kirst finally showed his age, going one for sixteen shooting.

The following day, Moran died. He was eighty-five. The tributes came quickly. A player who had tried out for the team in the halcyon 1970s days recalled in one of the opening drills, he stumbled on the new artificial turf inside Schoellkopf Field and fell on his face; not surprisingly, Stuart Binstock was cut from the team. The surprise came later. Binstock says for years and years after, Moran remembered him by name, also correctly recalling Binstock was living in Maryland; Moran never failed to ask Binstock about his family and job. Another story was the high school standout who, in the 1970s, selected Johns Hopkins over Cornell. Seeing Moran at a function many years later, he introduced himself, adding, "You probably don't remember me," to which Moran replied, "Don't remember you? I remember your SAT scores!" "Everybody wants to be friends with the popular people in life," says Buck Briggs, a 1976 Cornell alum and close friend of Moran. "My mom—a creature of a different era—used to say, 'The quarterback on the football team or the captain of the cheerleaders.' It is more important to reach out and befriend the people who need a friend. That is the true sign of who you are as a human being. I will think about Richie forever, but, more important, I will try to emulate him as a caring person who reached out to everybody, regardless of their station in life."

Moran's family delayed his funeral until early June, after the lacrosse season. Moran was survived by his wife of sixty-one years, Pat; three children; and eight grandchildren. The last game he ever saw at Schoellkopf Field was the one in which his grandson scored three goals, known as a hat trick. Sposito had never scored a hat trick before that mid-April Saturday in his native Ithaca. In his final two years at Army, which included an extra year of eligibility, he didn't score one again.

The Big Red ended the 2022 regular season with a game at Princeton, one week after the loss to Brown, days after Moran's death, and coming off a rare three-day break from lacrosse, a gift from the coaches to players who seemed and sounded jaded. Prior to that game, there had not been much talk of the NCAA tournament nor of making a deep run into May. Before the game in the Class of 1952 Stadium, Adler delivered a brief message. "This group is special," he said. "Let's keep playing for as long as possible, for as much time together as possible." The game began, and Adler took over. He finished with eight groundballs and five caused turnovers. Cornell won, 18–15. A loss in the Ivy League semifinals to Yale did not derail the momentum. One year after having their season canceled, the Big Red qualified for the eighteen-team NCAA tournament, one of six Ivy League teams to do so.

Cornell, given a number seven seed, was set to host Ohio State in the first round. Undefeated Maryland received the number one overall seed. Cornell's players normally wear their Teagle T-shirts under their jerseys. For the 2022 NCAA tournament, they wore something different. The T-shirts they chose were sometimes red, sometimes white, and read "Cornell Lacrosse" on the front and, on the back, the words "It's great to be here!—Coach Moran."

On Sunday, May 15, in the early stages of the Ohio State first-round game, it was not great to be at Schoellkopf Field. The game was delayed one hour by lightning. Then the Buckeyes jumped to a 4–0 lead. Early in the second quarter, with Cornell trailing 4–2, there was another lightning delay, this one lasting ninety minutes. In the home locker room, Stevens, unhappy the defense had given up four goals in little more than a quarter, had sharp words for Doria. Particularly, he wanted the four-year starter to follow the game plan when Ohio State had the ball behind the goal and was looking for a pass to an off-ball cutter for a quick, high-percentage shot. "We call that defense 'Ranger,'" Doria says, "and Coach Stevens was telling me, 'You've got to be better.'" Stevens showed a video clip from earlier in the game, of Doria's stick down by his side rather than in a passing lane, as prescribed in Ranger. The game resumed. Three or four times, when Ohio State had possession behind the goal, Doria remembered Stevens's words and put his stick high in the air. He knocked down a couple passes, then intercepted one for a caused turnover.

On offense, Kirst entered having been held without a goal in the Ivy League semifinal loss. Ohio State held him scoreless in the first quarter. Then, in a span of around thirty-three minutes, Kirst scored seven goals, showing his penchant for following a poor performance with a superlative one. Cornell won, 15–8. After the game, the seniors resumed their tradition of meeting in the room of classmate Luca Tria in his off-campus house in Collegetown. They had met there after every game, win or lose, to have a couple drinks and discuss the game in granular detail. After beating Ohio State, and with the weather delays, they arrived in Tria's room in time to catch the latter stages of the final first-round game between unseeded Delaware and second-seeded Georgetown; the winner would face Cornell. The Blue Hens, coached by former Cornell coach Ben DeLuca, pulled off a 10–9 upset. "We knew it wouldn't be a cakewalk," Doria says. "But you could feel the confidence growing around us." The freshmen felt it, too. They watched Delaware's upset victory from their townhouses on the North campus. "The freshmen all looked at each other," says Michael Bozzi, "and said, holy shit, we're one winnable game from playing on Memorial Day Weekend."

The optimism also stemmed from the emergence of senior Adler, a unanimous pick for first-team All-Ivy. He was a true shutdown defender and drew Delaware's leading scorer in Columbus, Ohio. Cornell won, 10–8, proving once again a maxim from Hall of Fame coach Bill Tierney: If adding the face-off win percentage and the goalie save percentage equals one hundred or more, your team is very likely to win the game. Against the Blue Hens, in practically empty Ohio Stadium, game balls went to Petrakis, for his fifteen-for-nineteen performance on face-offs (79 percent), and Ierlan, who made fifteen saves and gave up eight goals (65 percent). Adler also won his matchup, holding the Blue Hens' main threat to no goals and one assist. The Big Red advanced to Championship Weekend in East Hartford, Connecticut. The second quarterfinal in Columbus was a rematch of the 2021 title game, Virginia against Maryland. The undefeated, top-seeded Terrapins jumped to leads of 4–1, 9–3, and 15–5 en route to an 18–9 victory. Afterward, Virginia Coach Lars Tiffany sounded the alarm. "We just faced," he told reporters, "in my opinion, the best team in the last sixteen years."

The semifinals were set, a doubleheader on Memorial Day weekend, Cornell against Rutgers followed by Maryland against Princeton. In the mid-1980s, the NCAA tweaked its tournament format. For ten years, the semifinals had been played at the home stadium of the higher seed. The home teams went a combined 20–0. Fearing a competitive imbalance, in 1986 the sport installed a Final Four format, largely modeled on the NCAA's successful basketball tournament. The semifinals and final would be played at the same location, a neutral site, on Memorial Day weekend, semifinals on Saturday, title game on Memorial Day. The first iteration, in 1986, took place in Newark, Delaware. Fifth-seeded North Carolina upset top-seeded Johns Hopkins, followed by number-three Virginia outlasting number-two Syracuse. A tradition was born.

Cornell had its eye on Rutgers for much of the 2022 season, though not through any prescience. It was because the Rutgers star goalie was senior Colin Kirst, brother of Cornell's CJ. Rutgers was in the semifinals for the first time in program history. It entered having beaten a pair of Ivy League teams, Harvard in the NCAA first round and Penn in the quarterfinals. In those games, Kirst made thirty-five saves and gave up only eighteen goals. On offense, the Scarlet Knights liked to set picks, then hope for a mix-up on the defense to lead to an open shot. Cornell's defensive plan was to be aggressive on the picks, to not sit back and let Rutgers have a clear moment or two to decide whether to pass or shoot. The star Scarlet Knight was attackman Ross Scott, 5-feet-9, 175 pounds, a native of West Linn, Oregon, speedy with a hard outside shot. In the NCAA first-round victory over Harvard, Scott scored eight goals. Bartolotto recalled overhearing a coaches' meeting days before the semifinal. One of the coaches brought up jersey number five, meaning Scott. Defensive coordinator Stevens gave a quick answer: "I have Gavin [Adler] on him. He'll be neutralized. Let's move on."

Cornell traveled to East Hartford for a walkthrough practice the day before the game, then headed to its hotel, the Marriott in downtown Hartford on Columbus Boulevard. Around thirty minutes before the team dinner, Buczek asked Doria if he wanted to deliver the traditional night-before-the-game speech. "I mostly talked about the Long Red line," Doria says. "About the 2020 class that didn't get to play again, the opportunity we had that they didn't get to have. I reminded them of the work we had done to get here, the conditioning with Coach Howley. And I also said, don't forget to play loose and relaxed. Have fun." That night, according to *Lacrosse Magazine*, CJ Kirst did a quick FaceTime call with Colin. The two joked about which color cleats the Ivy League rookie of the year should wear. The brothers did not need reminders about having fun on the field.

On Saturday, the crowd of 21,668 included hundreds of Cornell students, fans, and lacrosse alumni, many of whom reminisced in the grassy tailgate area about the late Moran. One Cornell student brought a sign into the game noting the Kirst family's divided allegiance: "CJ is the favorite child!" Trailing 1-0, Kelleher, on his typical hard-dodge to the goal, was so forceful he bent the stick of defensive midfielder Brendan Kamish, who raced off the field to get a new one. Another Kelleher dodge later in the quarter knocked a defender clean off his feet. By the end of the first quarter, each member of Cornell's starting attack—Piatelli, Kirst, and Long—scored an unassisted goal, and Cornell led 3-1. The goal by Kirst gave him fifty-one on the season and was his seventy-third point, breaking the school record for points by a freshman set by Teat in 2017.

The Big Red extended the lead to 8-3 at halftime, at which point dangerous thunderstorms swept into the area, accompanied by forty mile per hour winds and hail. Resuming play was impossible. Fans were told, over the loudspeaker and on video boards, to exit the stadium. Cornell and Rutgers remained in their locker rooms. Princeton and Maryland, en route to the stadium for the second semifinal, headed back to their hotels. The bad weather caused thousands of homes in Connecticut to lose power. Amtrak faced hours of delays after the electrical storms damaged its tracks near New Haven. In the Cornell locker room, the coaches and players watched film, stayed hydrated, and examined changes and tweaks for the second half. Howley told the team to trust in its training, trust in each other, and let instinct guide them.

After a delay of three hours and thirty-five minutes, Cornell and Rutgers resumed their game. Early in the third quarter, Kelleher scored an unassisted goal, then ran into a Rutgers defenseman with such force he bent that stick as well; the goal gave the Big Red a 10-4 lead. Later in the quarter, a photographer from *Lacrosse Magazine* snapped a photo of Colin Kirst leading a clearing attempt amid heavy pressure from CJ. Both brothers had huge smiles. (And this was *after* the three-plus-hour delay.) The fourth quarter was largely anticlimactic. Cornell won, 17-10, thanks to five goals from Piatelli, four from Long, and three from Kirst and Kelleher. Adler won his matchup as well, holding Scott to one goal and two assists. As the game ended, the first player to commiserate with Colin Kirst was CJ, giving him a handshake and a hug as a startled Rutgers defender, intending to do the same, took a step backward. The game started at 12:05 p.m.; with the delay, it ended at 5:45 p.m. The NCAA requested thirty-five minutes for warmups before the second semifinal.

Finally, at 6:28 p.m., Princeton's Tyler Sandoval and Maryland's Wierman met at the midfield line for the opening face-off for the second semifinal. The Terrapins led 7–3 late in the first half when one of its defenders was called for a three-minute nonreleasable penalty. Princeton scored on extra-man offense to close to 7–4 at halftime. Momentum swung against the top-seeded team. Maryland fought back and won 13–8, but the game ended at 8:44 p.m. and required more energy than the early stages proffered. It compounded Maryland's already compressed schedule for Monday's 1 p.m. title game—unable to be pushed back because of the ESPN television schedule—and different from the regular season, when teams normally have a week to prepare. Maryland Coach John Tillman and a handful of players stayed behind for interviews with the media. Tillman was delayed further with the NCAA's mandatory random drug-testing policy for participating teams. Officials selected a sophomore reserve attackman who was so dehydrated he was having trouble providing a sample. The night stretched further. Finally, with the drug test over, Tillman and the remaining players and coaches made their way back to the downtown Marriott, the same hotel as Cornell.

The weather delay and long semifinal Saturday seemed little more than a speed bump. The undefeated Terrapins (17–0) entered the championship game with a remarkable résumé. They ran roughshod over lacrosse, a 22–7 victory over Johns Hopkins, a 23–12 regular season win over Virginia, a 17–7 regular season win over Final Four participant Rutgers, and an 18–9 quarterfinal win over Virginia. The Terrapins treated the sport's bluebloods with a dismissive swipe left like on a dating app.

The offense revolved around fifth-year senior Logan Wisnauskas, 6-feet-3, 215 pounds, a transfer from Syracuse, a onetime high school quarterback from Baltimore, Tewaaraton Trophy winner, and first-team all-American attackman. He was so committed to lacrosse he logged off social media during the season, so humble that he spent an hour once a week throwing and catching a lacrosse ball against a brick wall, a workout he called "Wallball Wednesday," something so spartan and simple not even high school players feel compelled do it in-season. Wisnauskas entered the title game with fifty-nine goals and forty assists. Fifth-year senior Anthony DeMaio was the all-time leading scorer in California high school history, with 391 points for Coronado High. He entered the title game having scored three goals in the Big Ten semifinal against Johns Hopkins, four goals in the conference title game win over Rutgers, and three goals in each of the NCAA first-round and quarterfinal wins. Senior Owen Murphy, considered surplus to requirements by the new coaching staff at Johns Hopkins, reemerged at Maryland as an unerringly dangerous sidearm shooter and scored thirty-four goals. The starting midfield featured Donville, the former Cornell captain who was so unenthused to face his former team months earlier, in the fall scrimmage at Delbarton. The stakes this time were significantly higher. He entered the title game with thirty goals. Wierman, the face-off specialist from West Chester, Pennsylvania, was on a mission given how the previous year ended. He entered the championship winning 66.1 percent of his face-offs and having set a school record with 272 face-off wins. Like Wisnauskas, he was a first-team all-American, along with defenseman Brett Makar and shortstick defender Roman Puglise.

Amid the cavalcade of talent, one other player caught Cornell's eye—junior Logan McNaney, the starting goalkeeper. He had been raised in tiny Cortland, New York, population 10,667, and his father played college lacrosse as a defenseman; his mother started the girls' program at Corning East High. McNaney, at 5-feet-8, 170 pounds, excelled with quick hands and a calm mind. Sheehan faced McNaney in an all-star tryout in Central New York in 2019. "I had a stepdown shot from 10 yards, dead center of the field," Sheehan says. "I shot as hard as I could and placed it perfectly, low and away. Unfortunately for me . . . Logan made a one-handed save and caught it like it was the easiest thing he'd ever done. Needless to say I never liked facing him." His Maryland teammates said after giving up a goal, whether it was his fault or that of a defender, McNaney sometimes responded by telling a joke to lighten the mood. In the day and age of hip-hop and dance music, McNaney told *The Baltimore Sun* his pregame favorites were AC/DC, Metallica, and Led Zeppelin, a classic rock playlist inspired by his father.

McNaney's star turn came in the 2021 semifinal against Duke. The Blue Devils entered with two first-team all-Americans on offense, plus attackman Brennan O'Neill, so promising a prospect he was considered the best high school player on talent-rich Long Island starting in his sophomore year. Against this array of talent, McNaney gave up five goals and made seventeen saves. The Terrapins won in a blowout. One year later, in the weather-delayed semifinal against Princeton, McNaney made nineteen saves, giving up seven goals (Princeton's eighth score came against a reserve).

Tillman prepped his team for Memorial Day 2022 and Cornell by telling them the following: They had a really good sense of who they were and who they wanted to be. They went out and played that way. They had a really good sense of self, a strong sense of identity. The coaches reinforced it, and the players bought into it. Top to bottom, everyone understood what they were doing and were pulling in the same direction. Tillman was perhaps more familiar than most; he had played for Moran and graduated from Cornell in 1991.

CHAPTER 3

The morning of the title game, Doria and sophomore reserve goalkeeper Walker Wallace boarded an elevator at the downtown Marriott. The doors opened for another passenger. Noting the lacrosse players' attire, he gave out a loud, "Are you going to win the big game!?" Doria replied, "I don't know, I'm just thinking about breakfast." The moment might have ended there, if not for Wallace. He burst into the meal and told the team about the interaction. Wallace found it the encapsulation of the program's mantras—control the controllables, focus on the inputs, let the outcomes take care of themselves. ("I'm not normally that stoic," Doria says now. "I don't even know where that came from.") The rest of the players gloried in it. Cornell was hours from facing undefeated Maryland, with its four first-team all-Americans—only Adler made the list for Cornell—on national television and before a crowd of more than twenty thousand people, all while trying to end a forty-five-year national title drought while honoring a beloved longtime coach who died weeks before. First, though, came breakfast.

The inaugural NCAA lacrosse tournament, in 1971, ended with a Maryland-Cornell matchup. The crowd that first Saturday of June at Hofstra University Stadium was good, 5,458 people, but it was not a sellout, and not even the best-attended game of the weekend. Army-Navy the following day in Annapolis, played in the first week of June as part of commencement festivities, drew more than ten thousand fans. The first title game was not broadcast on TV except by Baltimore's NBC affiliate, and even that was down to serendipity, as Cornell's backup goalie was the son of the station manager. The trappings in place fifty-one years later made the event unrecognizable. It was broadcast live on ESPN— "it's the undefeated against the undaunted," thrilled Anish Shroff in the opening. More than twenty-one thousand fans made their way to Pratt & Whitney Stadium. The teams stood at attention for the national anthem on a sunny, warm day with a breeze. As the anthem began, local students unfurled a giant American flag, taking up a decent part of the playing surface. As the anthem ended, three Army Blackhawk helicopters flew overhead, low enough to be very loud, and fireworks burst into the sky.

By this point, the talented Puglise, dealing with a significant hand injury, had received permission from doctors to play, with a codicil: He was not to attempt a pass, nor try to catch one; he was only to play defense with his quick feet while checking defenders, leading with his noninjured hand. Tillman took the field Monday wearing a baseball cap with the black RM sticker, in honor of Moran.

The game began, Adler guarding Wisnauskas, Makar on Kirst. Midway through the first quarter Kirst dodged against Makar and beat McNaney with a righty, off-hand shot for the opening goal. Later, McNaney saved a shot from Kirst, then one from starting midfielder Matt Licciardi, then made two saves on shots by midfielder Billy Coyle, then another on a shot by Licciardi. At the other end, Maryland was having success. DeMaio had a hat trick in the first quarter alone. The quarter ended Maryland 4, Cornell 1; McNaney made six saves. The second quarter began. McNaney picked up where he left off, saving a shot from Kelleher, then Kirst. At halftime, Maryland led 7–2, and McNaney made ten saves. "He was unreal," Kelleher says of the Maryland goalkeeper. "He had our number for sure." In the locker room, Cornell's coaches reminded the players of the off-season workouts, the Thursday nights when they had to do their maximum weight on the squat exercise, then woke up on Friday for a 6:30 a.m. one-mile, full-sprint run. The main strategic change was a call for the offense to take higher-quality shots, to be patient if needed. In the stands in East Hartford, old-timers recalled the 1976 title game, Cornell against Maryland, and the Terrapins holding a 7–2 halftime lead.

In the third quarter, Maryland extended the lead to 9–2. Cornell's offense kept its spirits up. "We brought it in and said okay, team offense, let's go," Kelleher says. "Let's keep looking for the best shots." By this point, Piatelli, the leading scorer in the nation, not guarded by Maryland's best defender, was scoreless and had taken only two shots. His third shot, late in the third quarter, was a goal. Entering the fourth quarter, the Big Red trailed 9–3. The Big Red went to a ten-man ride, a version of basketball's full-court press. Maryland, with Puglise under orders not to try to throw nor catch, was thus not an option to receive an outlet pass and clear the ball. Essentially, Maryland was trying to clear with nine people against Cornell's ten. The momentum swung. Long scored to close the deficit to 9–4, then Kelleher scored for 9–5, then reserve Spencer Wirtheim made it 9–6. Maryland's offense committed three consecutive turnovers, its players starting to cramp and show signs of fatigue and dehydration. With the quick turnaround from Saturday and Cornell playing with confidence, the game grew tighter. With three minutes and thirty-two seconds to play, Piatelli scored an apparent goal that was wiped out for a crease violation. It would have closed the deficit to two goals. In the final minute, Cornell called a time-out. In the Maryland huddle, defensive coordinator Jesse Bernhardt reminded his players Cornell liked to use a set-piece out of time-outs, essentially a pick-and-roll. Play resumed. Cornell went to its pick-and-roll. Neither defender followed Piatelli, who scored on an assist by Kirst. Thirty-six seconds remained. Wierman finished his revenge tour by winning the ensuing face-off. Cornell's threat, and season, ended. Maryland won, 9–7.

After the game, Tillman and Bernhardt asked Piatelli's defender what had happened on the pick play. "My legs were gone," he replied. "I was too tired." The star was McNaney; he made seventeen saves, many of them on shots within five yards. Kirst led Cornell with two goals and an assist, and Adler led a defense that, facing one of the best teams in the sport's recent history, did not give up a goal in the final twenty-six minutes. Cornell left the field one last time, in its tight-twos formation, the scene captured in a photo that Sheehan later committed to memory. In San Francisco, early on that Memorial Day morning, a former Cornell lacrosse commit watched the title game on TV. Duke Reeder was entering his sophomore year playing football at Stanford, as an outside linebacker and defensive end. "I knew Maryland was really good, one of the best ever," Reeder says. "I was like damn, Cornell came pretty close. . . . It was such a tease for the program over the years, 2009, 2013, all those title games and Final Fours [Cornell] lost in crazy fashion."

Bartolotto recalled working during his COVID-enforced time at home, doing an internship and then taking a job landscaping to make extra money to help pay tuition and be back with the team in 2022. The year led to fourteen victories, an appearance in the national title game, and a chance to mold the next group of Cornell players. "I thought losing the 2021 season was the worst thing that ever happened to me," Bartolotto says now. "It wound up being the best thing that ever happened to me." LaFalce, in attendance that day, remembers thinking Cornell had been closer to ending its streak than some might have realized. "If that Maryland game were five minutes longer," he says, "I think Cornell wins."

4

THE WANDER YEARS

Amid the disappointment of losing the 2022 NCAA final was a sliver of good news. So many of the players who took the field for Cornell that day had eligibility until 2025. Sophomore CJ Kirst, with powerful dodging from his 6-foot-1, 190-pound frame, created shots for himself almost at will. A college all-American attackman from the 1980s, a onetime high school coach and close observer of the sport, marveled at how Kirst was strong enough to get into the parts of the field he wanted to go to and release shots even with constant attention from defenders. Kirst finished 2022 with fifty-five goals.

Kelleher, the hard-running midfielder from Long Island, added twenty-three goals. The second-line midfield included freshman Alex Holmes (four goals, three assists) and sophomore Ryan Sheehan (three goals, including one in the semifinal win over Rutgers), with freshman Andrew Dalton earning a spot in the rotation for the title game. Freshman Danny Caddigan (three goals) became a mainstay on extra-man offense, though he did not appear in the title game because the Terrapins were not called for a penalty. The shortstick defenders included regulars Chris Davis (twenty-eight groundballs, four caused turnovers) and Michael Bozzi (three groundballs), both freshmen, and sophomore Kyle Smith (six groundballs). Freshman Jayson Singer (nine groundballs) bounced between close defense and longstick midfield and appeared in all four NCAA tournament games. One other intriguing prospect was junior Michael Long, the quarterback of the offense with eligibility until 2025, thanks to being part of two COVID-related cancellations. Long finished 2022 with thirty-four goals and thirty-two assists and led the team in shooting percentage (47.8 percent).

Another move that skewed toward the young came soon after the 2022 title game, when Cornell removed the interim tag from Connor Buczek's title; the national search had gone no further than the current coaches' offices. Buczek was born outside Cincinnati, Ohio, the oldest of three, though his family has roots in New York—both his parents are from the Buffalo area. Gary Buczek was a lacrosse and football team captain at Orchard Park High and played football at Rutgers as a defensive back. Buczek's mother, Mary, attended Nardin Academy, a small, academically rigorous all-girls Catholic school, and then St. Mary's College in Indiana. Gary Buczek earned his MBA from Notre Dame, and the couple got married and settled in Cincinnati. Connor Buczek's introduction to lacrosse came as a child, during a summer visit to see family in Buffalo. His parents signed him up for a lacrosse camp at Orchard Park High run by legendary coach Gene Tundo. Upon returning to Cincinnati, Buczek asked to join a youth league. The setup of Cincinnati youth lacrosse in the early 2000s was so haphazard there were no age groups. It meant Buczek, then in second grade, began his career playing against sixth graders.

For high school, Buczek attended St. Xavier, an all-boys Jesuit school with an enrollment of around 1,300 students. It is something of a powerhouse in sports, with numerous alums going on to play in college. Even in this crowded landscape, Buczek distinguished himself. He grew to 6-feet-2, 200 pounds, and was a two-year letter winner in football as a defensive back. The first game of his senior year in 2010 was a showdown against nationally ranked Good Counsel (Maryland), broadcast by ESPN. While helping defend future NFL wide receiver Stefon Diggs, Buczek made eight tackles in a game his team led for three quarters before losing, 21–6. He finished the year with eighty-two tackles, two sacks, and an interception. In the classroom, Buczek maintained a 4.0 grade-point average. Yet it was lacrosse where he truly stood out. Buczek was a four-year starter on attack. He finished his career with 410 points, believed to be an Ohio record. In a playoff game against Elder (Ohio) in 2011, his senior season, Buczek scored ten goals. His high school coach told the *Cincinnati Enquirer*, "Connor was virtually unstoppable." Buczek drew the attention of numerous colleges. Syracuse was an ardent suitor, believing his speed and size would be perfect for its up-tempo style. Cornell, too, recruited him hard. He committed to Cornell after his junior year, then visited for the season opener of the 2011 season against Hobart, a chance to see the team and meet with Coach Ben DeLuca.

Also in attendance that day, in late February 2011, with temperatures in the mid-twenties and snow piled high off the field, was a defensive commit from Long Island. Jordan Stevens grew up in Smithtown, New York, on the same street as Cornell star Rob Pannell. It was through Pannell that Stevens began to consider attending Cornell. "Cornell was completely unknown for me outside the Pannells," Stevens says. "My whole life I wanted to go to Hofstra. That was going to be my comfort zone. Cornell was outside of my comfort zone." He and Buczek met for the first time at the Cornell-Hobart opener. The pair, with their fathers, both named Gary, wound up watching the game together, among the hardy announced crowd of 512 at Schoellkopf Field. The four then repaired to the iconic Collegetown Bagels for a late lunch. "It's not like now, with social media, and you know who everyone is," Stevens says. "With Connor it was more like, I'm coming to Cornell, and he said so am I." They arrived in Ithaca in the fall of the 2011–12 academic year, part of the group of freshmen living in townhouses a couple doors down from each other. The first day on campus, Buczek offered to drive Stevens to the locker room in Schoellkopf Field, to drop off their lacrosse equipment. As he backed out of his parking space at the stadium, Buczek slammed into a tree. "We'd been on campus 30 minutes, and he'd already gotten into an accident," Stevens says.

As freshmen in the 2012 season, Stevens and Buczek were even close to each other in the game program, Buczek wearing jersey number 33, Stevens wearing number 35. Stevens was an immediate starter. At 6-feet-1, 180 pounds, with quick feet and incredible stickwork, he started the first six games on close defense and played in all thirteen. DeLuca moved Buczek to midfield, to better take advantage of his athleticism. The adjustment was slow. Through March and April Buczek took one shot, an attempt in the final five minutes against Canisius that was saved. The excellent student also struggled in the classroom, by his own admission, and from the blows to his ego, going from record-setting attackman to reserve midfielder. Buczek finished his freshman year with one goal, scored in the finale against Yale, a season-ending loss in the Ivy League tournament semifinals.

As sophomores in 2013, Stevens and Buczek were in the starting lineup for the season opener against Hobart inside the Carrier Dome. Buczek scored four goals in a 19–11 victory. Thus began a year where the close friends flourished, along with star attackman Rob Pannell, back for a fifth year. Buczek scored four goals against Syracuse, then another four in a victory over Princeton. In an NCAA first-round victory over Maryland, Stevens had five caused turnovers. In the quarterfinals, Cornell crushed Ohio State, 16–6, and was a prime pick to win its first title since 1977. In the NCAA semifinals against Duke in Philadelphia, a goal by Pannell gave Cornell a 6–5 lead with around two minutes left before halftime. Duke scored the next nine goals. Late in the third quarter, it led 14–6. Cornell battled back. It closed to 15–14 on a goal by Buczek with fifty-three seconds to play. The huge crowd of Cornell fans rose to their feet. The Blue Devils won the ensuing face-off and scored the clinching goal in a 16–14 victory. Buczek finished the season with thirty-five goals, and Stevens added twenty-three caused turnovers. Pannell finished with forty-seven goals and fifty-five assists and won the Tewaaraton Trophy as the sport's top college player. He finished his career with 354 points, then an NCAA record. But he did not win an NCAA title.

In November 2013, DeLuca was dismissed as head coach. The reason was not given publicly, but it came a few weeks after an alleged hazing incident forced the team to cancel its fall scrimmage. Cornell was still reeling from the death, two years earlier, of a student in alcohol-related fraternity hazing. "There is no doubt," Cornell's athletic director said in a statement announcing DeLuca's departure, "new leadership is needed." Many alums were significantly north of furious. They saw in DeLuca a Cornell alum and the last coaching tie-in to the on-field success and cultural breakthroughs of Dave Pietramala and Jeff Tambroni. He was one of their own. Moreover, he had just taken the team to the Final Four, and the cancellation of fallball and the fall scrimmage in Bethesda, Maryland, was a significant punishment. Hundreds of lacrosse alums, parents of former players, and supporters signed a letter protesting DeLuca's ouster.

Others were relieved DeLuca was gone. They found him gruff and off-putting, an unworthy successor to the largesse of Moran, the aura of Pietramala, and the sheer force of will of Tambroni, as if DeLuca absorbed all their negative qualities and none of the positive. Still others applauded the school's response to hazing allegations of all stripes. Into this hornet's nest stepped Cornell assistant Matt Kerwick, promoted to head coach. He was a hockey and lacrosse player at Hobart and longtime assistant on Georgetown's successful teams of the early 2000s. "It was hard," says Mark Wittink, Cornell lacrosse director of player development, Cornell lacrosse alum, Georgetown Law School graduate, and a member of the Cornell staff since 2012. "It was a house divided. Our alumni base is phenomenal, and very involved. There was a letter with hundreds of signatures of alums in support of Ben. It was a challenging couple of years bringing everybody back onto the same page."

This was the backdrop against which Stevens and Buczek entered their junior year in 2014, trying to keep the team together. The Big Red won its first nine games before faltering toward the end of the regular season. It reached the NCAA tournament and drew Maryland on the road in the first round. At halftime, Cornell led 5–1. In the second half, Maryland dominated face-offs and possession; Cornell took only eight shots and committed a handful of costly turnovers. The game was tied at 7 in the final seconds when Maryland scored the winning goal. Most disheartening was the manner in which Cornell lost. After the game, Maryland's goalkeeper described the toxic discussions he overheard. "They started to get frustrated at each other," Niko Amato said. "You could see out on the field that the attack was starting to grip their sticks and bicker at each other about slowing it down." Buczek was named first-team all-American and scored thirty goals. Stevens finished with fifty-two groundballs, the most by a non-face-off specialist. The early playoff exit did little to quell the frustration of losing DeLuca. Tempers frayed further when DeLuca reemerged as a volunteer assistant at Duke, took over the team's defense, and helped it win the 2014 NCAA title.

As seniors in 2015, Buczek and Stevens helped Cornell reach the NCAA tournament and host Albany in the first round. The Big Red opened perfectly, with goals on its first two possessions, from Buczek and senior John Hogan. The Great Danes scored the next eleven goals. Later came one of the most galling moments in Cornell's long NCAA tournament history. In the final seconds of the third quarter, with Albany leading by six goals, Hogan committed a turnover. Albany goalkeeper Blaze Riorden picked up the loose ball. With his team in total control, Riorden had little to lose and began running toward midfield. He crossed the midline, kept going, drew within fifteen yards of the goal, then fired a leaping, left-handed shot that beat Cornell's goalie. The score galvanized the Great Danes, embarrassed the Big Red, made the circuit of every possible televised sports highlights show, and shoved Albany on its way to a 19–10 victory. The final act of the college careers of Buczek and Stevens was to sit next to each other in the Schoellkopf Field media room, answering questions in a postgame news conference, even sharing an energy drink between answers. As luck would have it, Buczek sat in the middle, the spot often reserved for the head coach; Kerwick sat off to the side. And Buczek sounded every bit like someone in charge. "The game plan was to hold onto the ball, wear them down a little bit," he said, "then take a great shot instead of a good shot. We ended up settling for the good shot too often." Later, Stevens addressed his feelings on having played his final game. "I wouldn't trade what we have in those [locker room] walls for anything," he said. "For a [national title] ring, for a win today, two more wins down the road, I wouldn't trade it."

Buczek was named first-team all-American and left as the program's all-time leader for points by a midfielder, despite playing only three full seasons following his struggle to get into the lineup, or even the travel squad, as a freshman. Stevens made second-team all-American; both were named first-team all-Ivy, and Stevens also received a USILA scholar-athlete award. Stevens joked that from the time they got into the car as freshmen in late summer 2011 to drop off their equipment at Schoellkopf Field until graduation, he and Buczek had barely been more than fifteen feet apart. That was about to change.

In the fall of 2015, Stevens took a job at a hedge fund and moved to Manhattan. Buczek was accepted into Cornell's two-year MBA program. "It's hard to go directly into the Cornell MBA," says Tom LaFalce. "Most people doing that program have a few years' experience out in the workforce, then come back. That's not a program for people to go straight through from undergraduate." Buczek remained involved in Cornell lacrosse as a volunteer assistant. In 2016, his first year on the staff, Cornell went 6–7, including a 22–5 blowout loss to Brown. Defensive coordinator Chris Kivlen, Buczek's roommate in Ithaca, left to become head coach at a Division II program in North Carolina. A call went out to Stevens, then twenty-two years old, still regularly in touch. Would Stevens consider coming back to coach Cornell's defense, moving Peter Milliman to the offense? "We had a ton of staff turnover when I was in college," Stevens says, noting he was recruited out of high school by Tambroni and played for DeLuca and Kerwick. "Being one of the more experienced players, I kind of took a little bit more of a coaching role. It really piqued my interest, what a full-time coaching job would be like." Stevens gave his answer before Kerwick had hung up the phone. He was headed back to Ithaca.

In 2017, he reunited with Buczek, though seemingly not for long. At the end of the season, volunteer assistant Buczek earned his MBA and accepted a job in finance with JP Morgan. Then Kerwick, on the heels of a 5–8 finish, stepped down. "Matt is a great guy," Wittink says. "I have nothing but fond memories of him. But this program is not for everyone. It takes the right kind of person to manage a program with so many stakeholders. . . . It's not the kind of place where you can roll the balls out and just play freely. Our success is predicated on getting the right kind of kids, willing to subvert their individual interest for the collective goal."

Milliman took over, and Buczek rethought his plans. He wanted to coach lacrosse, but only at Cornell. Now, a full-time position as an assistant was available. Buczek canceled the finance job. Off the field, insiders like Wittink placed dozens and dozens of calls to disaffected alums, still rankled over DeLuca's dismissal. The program needed their support. DeLuca had landed on his feet, as head coach at Delaware. That chapter was over. Soon, the support from all corners reemerged. When Milliman left for Johns Hopkins in 2020, during the pandemic, only one of Stevens or Buczek could be named head coach. Then-athletic director Andy Noel proposed making them co-head coaches. The move, though well-intentioned, received immediate pushback. "You don't have co-generals," says Wittink. "Someone has to have the ultimate say. That was a hard decision for Andy. And I give so much credit to Jordan for how he handled it." Says Stevens: "It really came down to the two of us. The alums said it was really important that both of us stayed. Ultimately I'm really proud we worked it out. Admittedly, it was an interesting dynamic. But I'm proud we kept our relationship strong. The program took priority, and our friendship did not deteriorate." Buczek, too, acknowledges the difficult time proved fruitful. "We grew immensely as colleagues and friends," he says. "It was hard on its face to recognize it had to be one of us, it couldn't be both. . . . We grew into the roles together." With Buczek in tow, the last of the alums annoyed by the exit of DeLuca came back into the fold.

For the 2023 season, goalkeeper Chayse Ierlan decided to stay for his fifth year. Sophomore Wyatt Knust earned the backup spot largely through his relief appearance in the 2022 overtime victory over Syracuse. Now third string at best, junior Walker Wallace decided to ask about moving to defense, the position his older brother played for Cornell. The younger Wallace attended many of those games; while family and friends and alums were in the Crescent parking lot at the pregame tailgate, Walker, then in grade school, would squirrel into the third row of the bleachers and, notebook in hand, take notes on what caught his eye during warmups. (One entry began, "Coach Stevens waved to me!") It was also in grade school that Wallace wrote on a slip of paper the following note: "I will play Division I lacrosse." Every night for ten years, before going to bed, Wallace picked up the note and read it aloud. He attended St. Christopher's, an all-boys Episcopalian school in Richmond, the alma mater of noted author Tom Wolfe.

Wallace was spoiled for college choices. At 6-feet-6, 220 pounds, he had the size to play college football, basketball, or lacrosse. At St. Christopher's, he captained all three. As a senior in the 2019–20 academic year, he was first-team all-state in football, with 53 receptions for 522 yards and 8 touchdowns; all-league in basketball, averaging 10 points, 6 rebounds, and 3.3 assists; and an all-American lacrosse goalkeeper. Wallace boasted a 4.6 grade-point average, was a member of the Spanish Honor Society, an AP Scholar with Distinction, a student council member, and co-valedictorian. The slip of paper next to his bed in Richmond, Virginia, did not list any of those sports or academic programs as his college dream. So he committed to play goalie for Cornell.

After the 2022 season, the dream was a little more tricky. Wallace was on the team. Whether he'd actually play was in question. When he pitched the idea of switching positions to Kirst, one of his closest friends, Kirst began laughing. "We couldn't even say it with a straight face," Wallace says, Wallace decided to make the "crazy ask" of a position change. To make sure he didn't forget anything, Wallace wrote down a script, noting that he had played basketball in high school, and the footwork to play defense in lacrosse is similar. Soon after the 2022 title game loss, Wallace called his defensive coordinator. Stevens listened, then gave a quick answer: He, too, had thought about moving Wallace to defense. "It wasn't great to hear as a goalie recruit," Wallace says. "But it was good for my prospects for helping the team." Wallace acquired a defenseman's longstick and began the long path to learning a new position while playing at the highest level of Division I. The summer before the 2022–23 academic year, Wallace said, he was immersed in lacrosse seemingly twenty-four hours a day, either working out, throwing against the wall with a longstick, or watching highlights on his iPad. The long path to playing meaningful minutes had begun.

If it happened, it would be as a defensive midfielder. Spots on close defense were gone. The Big Red had senior Gavin Adler back, the best defenseman in the country; junior Jack Follows, a five-star recruit and 2020 Under Armour All-American; and Singer, who played valuable minutes as a freshman during the national title game run. Growing up in Syosset, New York, Singer's first love was basketball. He quickly realized that neither of his parents was taller than five-feet-nine. Basketball was not a likely path to play college sports. He began playing lacrosse in fourth grade—"for Long Island, that's pretty late," he says. "Most of my friends were playing in first and second grade." Singer caught up thanks to a family friend who had played for Division I Stony Brook and provided tutorials. Football was Singer's other favorite sport—he grew to 6-feet-1, 215 pounds, and he was a standout linebacker and running back. As a senior in 2021, he finished with 41 tackles and 7 tackles-for-loss, adding 585 rushing yards and 12 touchdowns. By this point, he also was a standout lacrosse recruit. "I loved football," he says. "But I couldn't turn down the places recruiting me for lacrosse." His final three schools were Cornell, Yale, and Virginia. Yale was coming off an NCAA title in 2018 and an appearance in the title game in 2019. Virginia was coming off beating Yale in the 2019 championship and would win the title again in 2021. Singer said the efforts of Stevens offset the on-field progress shown by the other programs. "He talked to my parents almost more than he talked to me," Singer said. "He built a strong relationship with all of us."

By the time the Big Red took the field for its 2023 opener, on the road against Albany, it had moved to number three in the USILA coaches poll and number two in the *Inside Lacrosse* media rankings. As in 2022, Cornell scored on its opening possession, a goal by senior Billy Coyle, one of the fastest players on the team. From there, the game became a struggle. The Great Danes led at halftime, 6–5; midway through the fourth quarter the game was tied at 9 on an extra-man goal by Albany freshman Silas Richmond; and it took late goals from juniors Dalton and Marc Psyllos to secure a 12–10 victory. Cornell won its next three games and kept its high ranking until early March and a 10–6 loss to Penn State in frigid Ithaca. By this point, an injured Long had yet to play; Kelleher, unstoppable at times, was mortal at others, and was shooting five for twenty-six (19 percent); and talented junior Aiden Blake, moved onto the first midfield line, was shooting two for twenty. Long came back after the loss to Penn State, moving into the starting attack, and Blake bumped to the main threat of the second line, as Sheehan moved into the starting midfield. That worked for a couple games, until early April and a 10–8 loss to Harvard in Cambridge, Massachusetts.

With the season seemingly on the brink, Cornell won a rare midweek matinee over Marquette, 20–15, before traveling to West Point, New York, to face Army. The Black Knights focused on stopping Kirst; not only did they assign their best defender to him, they also barred every shortstick defender from switching to cover Kirst after a pick or other off-ball machination. The ploy, to that extent, worked: Kirst finished with no goals, one assist, and a season-low five shots. Midway through the fourth quarter, the scoreboard suddenly went blank; the livestream over the internet did as well. After a ten-minute delay, play resumed, though still without a scoreboard nor working shot clocks nor a livestream. According to Matt Kinnear of *Inside Lacrosse*, the shot clock and game clock were kept by managers via stopwatches and cell phone timers on the sideline. In the final minute, the game was tied when Coyle threw a perfect cross-field pass to Blake, who scored on a quick shot. The players did not need the scoreboard to know the score gave the Big Red an 11–10 lead. It became apparent in the moments after Blake scored that only nine seconds remained in the game and three seconds on the shot clock.

The following week, on the road against Brown, Kirst again showed his penchant for following up a subpar game with a strong one; in a 16–9 victory he scored six goals, including two on overhand crank shots, from a low angle, using his right hand. Next came senior day at Schoellkopf Field, April 29. By this time the Big Red climbed back into the rankings, at number six. Princeton entered with sophomore Coulter Mackesy and his team-high forty-five goals. The next-highest player had scored eighteen. It was no secret he was the main scoring threat for Princeton, nor was it a secret who would guard him, as Adler drew the assignment. The Tigers led by a goal in the final minute when Blake scored to force overtime, then scored again for the winning goal in a 14–13 overtime victory. Mackesy finished with no goals, one assist, and only one shot. Adler countered with six groundballs and three caused turnovers. For all of the festivities of winning in overtime and claiming the Ivy regular season title, gameday began on a somber note. Around 150 people gathered for a morning ceremony honoring Moran. Several people spoke, including former Cornell players, Army junior Ryan Sposito—Moran's grandson, fresh off a game against Boston University the previous night—and Buczek. Then the Cornell glee club arrived to perform several Moran favorites, including "Felix the Cat" and "God Bless America." A bronze plaque with Moran's likeness and his achievements was unveiled outside the team locker room. "In a wheel of 1,000 spokes," it reads in part, "Richie was the hub."

Cornell was selected to the NCAA tournament as a number-eight seed and hosted Big Ten tournament champion Michigan in the first round. Kirst entered with sixty-three goals. The Big Red also had Adler, the best defenseman in the nation, and his fifty-nine groundballs and twenty-one caused turnovers. Long was back in the lineup and, in six games, scored twenty-two points. Even converted goalkeeper Wallace was contributing—he played twelve games as a longstick midfielder and scored two goals. Expectations were high. The winner would advance to play a quarterfinal at the University of Albany, less than three hours by car from Ithaca. The momentum from the 2022 title game run gave confidence to the Big Red faithful. All it would take was to defeat Michigan, playing in its first NCAA tournament game.

The back-and-forth contest at Schoellkopf Field featured ten ties, including at 14–all in the final seconds. Blake found himself with possession of the ball, six yards from the goal. Twice in recent weeks, Blake had scored the winning goal. Against Michigan, his shot clanged off the goalpost and bounced away, just inches from securing a spot in the second round. Instead the game went to overtime. ESPN's cameras panned the crowd of around three thousand; almost everyone was standing or nervously fidgeting. Many fans used their hands to cover their mouths in anxiety.

Cornell freshman Jack Cascadden won the opening face-off, taking the ball forward, an advantage made even more pronounced when the Michigan specialist stumbled. Cornell had a fast break. Cascadden, with one goal on the sunny afternoon, raced toward the Michigan goal. To his left, Coyle, three goals on the day, including the tying goal moments earlier on a running sidearm shot high into the net, suddenly popped open. Cascadden kept running. On the sideline, Buczek could have called a time-out to set up something more formal, perhaps for Coyle and his thirty goals on the season, maybe for Kirst and his sixty-five goals; instead, he kept his hands at his side. He would let his players make a play. Cascadden fired a hard, overhand shot from thirteen yards. Michigan goalkeeper Hunter Taylor made the save. Michigan cleared the ball and called a time-out.

The Big Red took the field with its starting close defense, plus freshman Brendan Staub at longstick midfielder and Davis and Bozzi as the shortsticks. Wolverines fifth-year senior Peter Thompson, Michigan native, born in Ann Arbor Hospital, the son of a Michigan professor, a transfer after spending four years as a reserve at Georgetown, initiated play, guarded by Staub. He swept the top of the offensive box, closely guarded by the freshman. The ball went to senior Michael Boehm, the quarterback. He drew a double team and passed to wide-open junior Isaac Aronson, who by this point was the focus of attention of several Cornell players, including Staub. Thompson, noting his defender was preoccupied, raced to the edge of the goalie crease. Aronson spotted him, threw him the ball quickly, and Thompson swept the ball past Ierlan. Cornell's season was over. Staub slammed his stick against his helmet, then fell to the ground. As a teammate tried to console him, Staub quickly walked away. A pair of Garden City High alums, Cascadden and Staub were classmates, teammates, and close friends from their days on the football and lacrosse teams at Garden City, inseparable to the point, Wittink says, that "if you see one of them, the other is usually not far behind." On May 14, 2023, they were united once again, this time in disappointment. When asked what he remembers from the game, Cascadden provides a typically honest answer. "I thought it was the best I played all year. Then In overtime I took a pretty shitty shot," he says, "and they came down and scored. It definitely burned. It definitely left a scar. It definitely gave me some motivation." Adler finished his career as Defenseman of the Year, first-team all-American, another certificate for the Schoellkopf Film room walls, but again no NCAA title.

For the 2023–24 academic year, Ryan Goldstein joined the ranks of Cornell lacrosse players as an incoming freshman. He had been wearing Cornell lacrosse gear for years. His father, Tim, was the standout attackman who eschewed a full scholarship from Hofstra to transfer to Cornell, play for the Southern Tier Lacrosse Club in 1986, then for the Big Red on the 1987 and 1988 national runners-up. Ryan Goldstein's mother, Tina Hennessey Goldstein, was a first-team all-American women's player at Cornell in 1992 and 1993. The athletic genes are deeper than the ties to Cornell. Hennessey's father was a star football player in the late 1950s at Brookline High in Boston. Tom Hennessey went on to play at Holy Cross. The first time he touched the ball, in the 1960 opener against Harvard, he returned the opening kickoff eighty-five yards for a touchdown. (Harvard came back to win, 13–6.) Nicknamed the Brookline Blur, Hennessey led the Crusaders to two victories over Boston College and later spent two seasons with the Boston Patriots in the American Football League, a precursor to the NFL's New England Patriots. Goldstein's great-great-grandfather hit the first home run in Fenway Park. Hugh Bradley turned the trick on April 26, 1912, six days after the stadium opened. Playing against the Philadelphia Athletics and a pitcher named Lefty Russell, Bradley blasted a shot over the left-field wall. On the one-hundredth anniversary of the home run, Ryan Goldstein and his family were on the field in Fenway Park to be honored. "I was kind of annoyed," Goldstein says. "I was in second grade, and that was the day of my teacher's birthday, and we always went outside and played a bunch of games. Looking back, I'm glad I was at Fenway instead."

Those athletic genes are just one side of the family. His uncle, Dennis Goldstein, was the star attackman in 1991 when North Carolina went undefeated and won the NCAA title. The families now live next door to each other in Radnor, Pennsylvania, outside Philadelphia, sharing a backyard. Within walking distance is the house of Mike French, Cornell all-American attackman, star on the 1976

NCAA title team. And Ryan Goldstein's godfather is Joe Lizzio, face-off specialist on the 1987 and 1988 Cornell teams. Goldstein was encouraged from a young age to play sports, lacrosse in particular, and Cornell was the dream destination. "Growing up, I went to almost every Cornell game," Goldstein says. "There wasn't really a different school I ever wanted to go to."

Goldstein committed to Cornell as a junior at Radnor High, coming off a season in which he had forty-four goals and forty-six assists and led the team to a Pennsylvania 3A state title. He is extremely quick—a good thing since he is 5-feet-9, 145 pounds, slender like a whippet. Wittink, doyen of Cornell lacrosse's voluminous social media endeavors, remembers seeing a picture of Ryan Goldstein dodging to the goal and noting the stance looked familiar. After a few minutes, it struck him—he went back to the files and found a photo of Tim Goldstein from 1987, striking almost the same pose. It can be hard for Ryan Goldstein to maintain weight because, from his youth, he has dealt with several food allergies, including eggs, shellfish, and dairy products like ice cream. Back home, his parents are his favorite chefs. When the Cornell team gathers for dinner the night before the game at the Statler Hotel on-campus, almost always chicken parmesan, pasta, and salad, Goldstein has to avoid it. When asked if he orders something different, he demurs. "It's hard, they're making dinner for 50 players and probably 70 people total, including coaches and staff," he says. "I don't want to be the one guy who asks for something different. I don't want to be a burden. Sometimes I just roll with the punches, and eat something afterward."

In the fall workouts in 2023–24, Goldstein was more of a burden to opponents than chefs. In a scrimmage against Maryland at Schoellkopf Field in mid-October, Goldstein scored three goals and Cornell won, 13–10. Fifth-year senior Michael Long missed the scrimmage; to maintain his eligibility, he was home for the fall semester. At the start of the spring semester, , the possibility of a Long-Kirst-Goldstein attack began to form. Then Goldstein broke his hand and missed several weeks. With Goldstein out, the third spot on attack went to junior Danny Caddigan, the extra-man specialist. He is the son of a decorated firefighter in the FDNY, at Engine 62, Ladder 32 in the Bronx, and the nephew of a decorated NYPD detective, Midtown South Precinct. The right-hander, 5-feet-9, 180 pounds, arrived in Ithaca after a storied career at Smithtown West High on Long Island. As a sophomore in 2019, he led Suffolk County with seventy-five goals. By September 1 of his junior year, he was unable to conduct many on-campus visits because of an ankle injury suffered while playing quarterback for the Bulls. His junior lacrosse season was wiped out by the pandemic. As a senior in 2021, Caddigan scored fifty-two goals. He originally committed to Colgate, to join an older brother playing there. The commitment was not yet binding. And Stevens, also graduated from Smithtown West, decided to make one last push. "His whole pitch was Cornell has a team full of guys like him and me," says Caddigan.

Another threat for the offense was Canadian freshman Willem Firth, considered by *Inside Lacrosse* to be a five-star recruit, and the number-nine overall prospect. His lacrosse star began to rise when he was six years old. In a youth tournament organized by the Nepean Knights indoor team based in Ontario, Firth's team went undefeated and scored thirteen goals. Eight came from Firth. He grew into a standout box lacrosse player, rising to the Junior A, the highest level for ages sixteen to twenty-one. In the summer of 2022, he became the first Toronto Beaches Junior A player to register a fifty-goal, one-hundred-point season. In the outdoor game, Firth starred at Hill Academy, Jeff Teat's alma mater. A 5-feet-10, 180-pound left-hander, he was recruited by several schools before selecting Cornell. With the lefty attack spot manned by Kirst, Firth was set to play midfield with Kelleher and fifth-year senior Spencer Wirtheim. The close defense was Follows, Singer, and Staub. Knust was the starting goalkeeper, and Cascadden was back as the primary face-off specialist, and with plenty of motivation. The Big Red began the 2024 season ranked fifth.

Cornell won its opener over visiting Lehigh, 17–13. The second game was against the University of Denver, on the road. On February 22, two days before the game, Cascadden suffered a significant knee injury in practice. He was out for the year. In stepped Marc Psyllos, senior from Manhasset, 5-feet-8, 190 pounds, and arguably the team's biggest personality. His pregame ritual was legendary: He would consume several energy drinks and multiple cups of coffee, an overload of caffeine. He was further famous for coming home from the lacrosse team workouts, then going back to the gym for more weightlifting. "Most of us were dead tired from those workouts, and he was going back out again. He was nonstop energy," says Kelleher. "I don't know if he ever slept." The game in Denver was as wild as Psyllos' metabolism. Firth scored four goals, Wirtheim, Kirst, and Caddigan scored three, and it wasn't enough. The Pioneers scored five extra-man goals in an 18–17 victory. In the game, junior Michael Bozzi, a starting shortstick defender, broke his collarbone; as the team flew home, he remained in the hospital, joined by his parents, for surgery the following day.

After victories over Hobart and Ohio State, the Big Red traveled to play Penn State. The typical watershed game was no different in 2024; by the end, Cornell would know what sort of team it had, what prospects were in store. The Nittany Lions scored the first four goals, then extended the lead to 6–1. At this point, freshman Matthew Tully replaced Knust. The onslaught continued. Penn State extended its lead to 10–1, then 18–6. The final score was Penn State 20, Cornell 9. The eleven-goal margin marked Cornell's worst since the 22–5 loss to Brown in 2016. The news went from bad to worse when Davis, the team's best shortstick defender, suffered a serious back injury, a herniated L5-S1 disc. He was out indefinitely. Cornell was set to face its Ivy League schedule without its two best shortstick defenders, arguably the most important position in lacrosse given that opponents target the SSDMs constantly. Teams can mitigate a weak shortstick defense by winning face-offs. This, too, was problematic, as Cascadden was out for the year, and the one-two punch was now just Psyllos.

Who would play goalie was another dilemma. Tully, from Foxborough, Massachusetts, was a five-star recruit, ranked marginally higher by *Inside Lacrosse* than even Firth. At this point, Knust was becoming his own worst enemy in trying to make up for the graduation of Ierlan. "I was putting a lot of pressure on myself," Knust says. "Looking back on it, I regret it. Every practice was super tense. I was trying to make every single save. I said I was trying to prove it to everybody on the team, but really I was trying to prove it to myself." Now, the Big Red had fallen to number fifteen in the rankings, and Knust was out of the lineup. The week of practice before the Ivy opener against Princeton was a low point. "I'd only been given the chance to start five games," he says. "And I didn't think I had played all that poorly. I understand Matty was playing great in practice, and I knew why the coaches wanted to give him a chance. I probably would have given him a chance, too. But not playing was very tough mentally." Knust, who had been watching film every day outside of practice, stopped doing so.

One bright spot came the week after the Penn State loss, in an Ivy League contest against Princeton. Goldstein, recovered from his preseason injury, was inserted into the lineup in the second quarter against Princeton in Class of 1952 Stadium. In less than two minutes he had an assist. Less than three minutes later, he had another. In the third quarter, he scored two goals and added another in the fourth. The 15–14 victory was clinched on a goal by longstick Matt Dooley with one second remaining. Goldstein was a revelation; in three quarters he finished with three goals and two assists, looking a bit like his father, whose Cornell debut in 1987 against Cortland State featured seven assists.

The season was finally looking up. For the following week against Yale, Goldstein moved into the starting lineup, replacing Caddigan, who remained on extra-man. Goldstein scored five goals, and Kirst added four goals and four assists, in an 18–15 victory. Knust, however, again put in a lethargic week of practice. After meeting with the coaches, he decided to change his outlook, learning from reading Jon Gordon's *The Hard Hat*, the seminal book on being a good teammate. "That wasn't the right way to handle it," he says. "I needed to mature and grow up. . . . The couple weeks I wasn't starting, and I was feeling down, and that wasn't going to do anything for me. The only chance I had to get back on the field was to be a good teammate and be positive. Showing up negative to practice and feeling down and not playing well, I knew my teammates wouldn't like it and the coaches would see it."

The rest of the season was up and down—an overtime loss to Penn, a double-overtime victory over Syracuse in which Knust returned and played well. By this point Davis was back in his home state of Vermont. The day before the Syracuse win, Davis had back surgery on his herniated disc. He was out for the season and possibly longer. The on-field roller coaster continued—a victory over Brown, a one-goal loss to national power Notre Dame. "We had battles with being consistent," Kelleher says. "We battled some injuries." Says Singer, "We didn't peak at the right time, which is what you want as a championship team. We were peaking in April, not May. Maybe we lost sight of the bigger picture, maybe we didn't have the consistency in practice. . . . Not being consistent in practice translates over to the games." The season ended in Ithaca, with blood on Kirst's jersey, a loss to Penn in the Ivy League semifinals, and the NCAA title drought at forty-seven years.

THE "21" YEAR

5

One other event came to define Cornell lacrosse, something far more significant than a national title drought. Richie Moran's successor, named in late August 1997, was Dave Pietramala, a three-time all-American defenseman at Johns Hopkins. He is considered one of the best in his position in lacrosse history and was at the forefront of the one loss in the Gait brothers' final three years at Syracuse; he shadowed Gary Gait in the season opener in 1989 in Baltimore, holding the star midfielder relatively quiet in the Blue Jays' 13–12 victory before ten thousand fans. (The teams met again in the 1989 title game in College Park, Maryland. The crowd of 23,893 fans included sitting Vice President Dan Quayle and his lacrosse-playing sons. Pietramala again held Gait in check, but this time Syracuse won by a goal.)

Pietramala arrived in Ithaca after three years as defensive coordinator at Johns Hopkins. He was a lifelong fan of college sports. His father was facilities manager at St. John's University, a position that gave his son ringside seats to the mid-1980s heyday of Big East men's basketball. Pietramala also was an avid college football fan, often visiting those programs for tips on practice and training and recruiting. While watching a college football game on TV in 1999, during fall workouts for his third season in Ithaca, Pietramala heard the commentators say the Virginia Tech defense used a lunch pail as a reminder to be tough and focused on the fundamentals and hard work. The Cornell coach borrowed the concept and conceived, rather than a lunch pail, a hard hat, to be given to a freshman each fall. It made its debut soon after the football broadcast and came to symbolize what Pietramala and assistants Jeff Tambroni and Ben DeLuca wanted from the players. As *The Cornell Daily Sun* put it, "The recipient is someone that the coaches feel demonstrates a blue-collar approach to the game of lacrosse; he is driven and selfless, not the most talented player on the field, but consistently the hardest worker. He puts the team first and embodies how the coaches want Cornell players to act and respond on or off the field."

The earliest iteration of the hard hat was white, with a C on the side outlined in black. The first winner in the fall of 1999 was J. P. Schalk, a midfielder from Fayetteville-Manlius High outside Syracuse. The recipient was charged with bringing the hard hat to every team event—practice, weightlifting, games at home and on the road, and so on. The hard hat dovetailed perfectly with Pietramala. He had a relentless, nonstop emphasis on recruiting—one story had him calling recruits on his honeymoon, and he was famous for sending handwritten letters to prized prospects, signing off with, instead of "Best Wishes" or "Fondly," the simple phrase "Win." The Big Red was showing signs of an upturn.

In 2000, the upturn arrived. Cornell had won six of its first seven games entering a midweek contest against number-one Syracuse. On a drizzly, chilly mid-April night in Ithaca, Big Red starting attackman Michael Egan, a freshman from Winnetka, Illinois, was benched for poor play. He reentered in the fourth quarter. In the final minutes he scored a goal to tie the game, then scored another to clinch a 13–12 victory. As the game ended, Cornell's players threw their sticks and gloves in the air and raced onto the field. It was the program's first victory over the number-one-ranked team since the 1976 NCAA final. If the hard hat was looking for endorsement, it received one that night. "Coach Pietramala has guys playing a little more physical than some of the Cornell teams in the past," Syracuse coach John Desko told reporters. "That is the attitude he is instilling in his team, and it is paying off."

The lacrosse world took note. This was especially true for a senior and honor roll student at Landon School in Bethesda, Maryland. George Boiardi was captain and running back-linebacker on the 1999 football team that won the Interstate Athletic Conference title; defenseman and forward on the hockey team that won the IAC tournament; and star longstick midfielder on the lacrosse team on its way to winning the IAC championship. He earned eleven varsity letters, making varsity in everything after the fall of 1996 and his stint on the freshman football team. Being a three-sport athlete is different from saying he made sports his primary focus. "He did it for the love of competition," says Teddy Lamade, a close friend, a teammate and classmate of Boiardi's at the youth level and in all three sports at Landon. "And to be with his teammates and friends. He seemingly had zero interest in following pro sports. . . . He was our star running back, and he barely knew who Emmitt Smith was." Added JR Bordley, a classmate, a teammate in football and lacrosse, and a close friend, "George was great in hockey, and I don't think he could tell you five guys who played for the Washington Capitals. I don't think he knew the names of five guys in the NFL."

Boiardi also had little care for accolades. Lamade remembers as freshmen in the spring of 1997, he and Boiardi were approached by Dave Kreter, the star quarterback, a senior headed to play football at Princeton. He invited the two freshmen to join an invitation-only leadership club, one of the more prestigious organizations at the all-boys private school. Lamade and Boiardi were the first two members of their class to receive an invitation. "Dave Kreter was kind of a role model for me. He was varsity quarterback, I was freshman quarterback," Lamade says. "I'm just glowing. It's a big honor. And after Dave walks away, George looks at me and says, 'What's that club?'"

As juniors at Landon in the fall of 1998, Boiardi, Lamade, and Bordley were on the field for the football game against local power Good Counsel (Maryland), with two future NFL players on its roster. The Bears, trailing by five points, scored a touchdown in the final minute to take the lead. Landon's coach opted for a two-point conversion attempt, for a three-point lead and insurance against a late field goal. The coaches called a toss sweep to Boiardi. He was tackled just short. Still, Landon led by one, though teammates noticed Boiardi was strangely quiet, different from the wild celebrations on the sideline. The Bears kicked off, Good Counsel took over on its own side of the field with seconds remaining. On first down, a long Hail Mary pass fell incomplete. After another pass fell incomplete, Boiardi turned around and asked why Good Counsel was throwing the ball when they had the lead. "He hadn't read the scoreboard," Bordley says. "A team like Landon never beats Good Counsel. It's one of the biggest wins I can remember. We were getting ready to dance on the field and George was inconsolable."

As a senior at Landon, Boiardi's college choices came down to Princeton and Cornell; he also made an official visit to Duke. When Pietramala and assistant Tambroni visited the Boiardi house in Washington, DC, they arrived for dinner. Pietramala noted George was quiet and asked if it was unusual. At this point his mother excused herself, went to her son's bedroom, and grabbed one of his prized possessions—a white paperweight with black letters, a Ben Franklin quotation: "Well done is better than well said." It was a trinket his father had found during a business trip to New York City. She placed the paperweight in front of the coaches. "This is how we live our life," she said.

George Boiardi visited the campus in Ithaca in the fall of 1999. According to the book *The Hard Hat*, he told friends he was impressed his host gave Boiardi his bed and slept on the couch. His official recruiting trip to Princeton, his father's alma mater, also came in the fall of 1999. It coincided with the visit of several highly sought-after prospects from Long Island. One of them, who later committed to Princeton, loudly asked the other recruits to watch his highlight video.

"That irked George beyond belief," says Lamade, also on the visit that weekend. "He would have thrown up at the idea of having a highlight film. The idea of making a highlight tape, let alone watching it, would have been abhorrent to him." The Long Island coterie knew each other from various all-star teams and immediately formed their own group. While watching practice in Class of 1952 Stadium, the Long Island contingent headed toward the press box at the top of the stands, laughing and making jokes, with no immediate outreach to the other recruits. Boiardi wanted to know more about Princeton's coaches and players and watched the drills intently, from the second row of the stands. He was joined by defenseman Tim DeBlois, from a Syracuse suburb, also not part of the Long Island hijinks. Princeton entered the 2000 season with five NCAA titles in eight years. Cornell won commitments from Boiardi and DeBlois. "Princeton was the pinnacle of college lacrosse then," Lamade says. "They had won five national titles in less than ten years. But Cornell felt like the right fit for him. Cornell already had that 'hard hat' mentality. And George was a hard hat guy."

DeBlois and Boiardi did not get to play for Pietramala. In the summer of 2000, fresh off being named Division I coach of the year and leading Cornell back to the NCAA tournament and a first-round loss to Georgetown, Pietramala accepted the head coaching job at Johns Hopkins. Cornell decided to keep the momentum as best it could by promoting offensive coordinator Tambroni to head coach. A few weeks later, Boiardi and the freshmen arrived. "George was an amazing teammate, and that's the highest praise in my book," says Scott Urick, an assistant in Tambroni's first year. "He loved his teammates and was the hardest-working kid we had. He never complained." Midway through the fall, coaches gave Boiardi the hard hat. He also was given jersey number 21, though the reasons behind it have been lost to history. Boiardi had worn number 24 in lacrosse at Landon. (In football at Landon, he wore jersey number 32; in hockey, he wore 39.) When Boiardi arrived at Cornell, jersey number 24 belonged to defenseman Chris Viola, a sophomore from Philadelphia. Numbers 23 and 22 also were taken. Urick believes in selecting number 21, Boiardi simply took the closest available number to 24.

Cornell's overall progress came slowly, then quickly. The Big Red had a solid season in 2001, with Boiardi named the team's freshman of the year. On returning home, Boiardi found his parents had placed many of the academic and athletic achievements on the wall of his bedroom in their house in Washington. He quietly took them down and put them back in the closet. In 2002, when Boiardi was a sophomore, Cornell won its first NCAA tournament game in years, a 12–3 first-round victory over Stony Brook. In 2003 Cornell shared the Ivy League title, its first time atop the conference in sixteen years, but was not selected for the twelve-team NCAA tournament. The snub provided motivation. A strong senior class was back in 2004. Midfielder Andrew Collins, from Yorktown, New York, led the '03 squad in scoring, with twenty goals and thirty-nine assists. Junior attackman Sean Greenhalgh, an excellent inside shooter from St. Catharines, Ontario, added thirty-seven goals and shot 43 percent. DeBlois, a starting defenseman, and senior Ryan McClay, a longstick midfielder from Mahopac, New York, each eclipsed fifty groundballs. McClay's excellence prompted the coaches to move Boiardi, a couple years earlier, from his preferred longstick midfield spot to shortstick defensive midfielder. Teammates said Boiardi did not complain. Instead, he picked up a shortstick and threw passes against a concrete wall to familiarize himself with the new equipment. "He wasn't the most skilled lacrosse player," says his father, Mario Boiardi. "But he was definitely the best athlete. And he worked out like mad."

In a further nod to Cornell's return to prominence, the NCAA awarded a 2004 quarterfinal doubleheader to Schoellkopf Field. Heady days were ahead. In December 2003, weeks before the preseason, Boiardi ran the forty-yard dash in 4.40 seconds, the fastest in program history. For the upcoming season Cornell would have four captains: DeBlois, Collins, junior defenseman Kyle Georgalas, and Boiardi. The move was years in the making. In lacrosse, Landon picked only one captain, and in Boiardi's senior year the honor went to Lamade. "Teddy was his best friend," says Mario Boiardi, George's father. "But George went to Cornell with the mission of being captain of the Cornell team."

Cornell began the season with victories in two of its first three games, though it was not yet playing as well as it wanted. Snow postponed the fourth game, against visiting Binghamton on March 16, by one day. On the morning of March 17, Boiardi had a job interview. His interest in Native American life and culture was piqued through classes at Cornell. After college he wanted to teach at the Red Cloud Indian School in Pine Ridge, South Dakota. The school, serving children of the Lakota Nation, dates from September 26–27, 1877, and the visit of a delegation led by Chief Red Cloud to the White House and President Rutherford B. Hayes. The group, with four interpreters, was welcomed into the spacious East Room, where years earlier Abraham Lincoln lay in state after his assassination; more recently it was the site of the wedding of Nellie Grant, daughter of then-President Ulysses Grant. Sitting in mahogany chairs, the group asked President Hayes for permission to build a school for Lakota children. A further request was for the school to be run by the Jesuits, present in the region for decades as missionaries but banned by Grant's administration from formal teaching duties.

One member of the delegation told President Hayes, "I would like to get Catholic priests. Those who wear black [robes]. These men will teach us how to read and write English." The president agreed. The project began. Construction was hastened considerably in the mid-1880s thanks to financing from Catherine Drexel, daughter of a wealthy family in Philadelphia who, visiting a friend in Nebraska, became fascinated with the Native American culture. (She later entered religious life and is now St. Katharine Drexel.)

In 1886, the school opened as Holy Rosary Mission, run by the Jesuits and the Lakota community. It became a site of teaching and learning, with a sad chapter: In December 1890, the campus served as a refuge site for those fleeing the massacre at Wounded Knee, less than ten miles away. Years later, and to honor its Native American founder, a convert to Catholicism, the school changed its name to Red Cloud Indian School. (Today it is known as Mahpiya Luta, the Lakota translation of the school's formal name.) Though the Jesuits remained heavily involved, Boiardi's interview on the morning of March 17 was with a group called Teach for America. Still, he was not taking chances. A family friend and Jesuit priest had spent a few years at Red Cloud School, and the priest recently moved across the street from the Boiardi family in the Spring Valley section of Washington. He and George had spoken earlier in the week about Red Cloud. It only furthered Boiardi's interest, along with Fr. Tim's offer to put in a good word, if needed. On March 17, the Teach for America interview went well, Boiardi told his inquiring friends. Teach for America later confirmed this to his parents.

Boiardi's plan to teach and help the Native American community was in place. He held onto the priest's phone number, just in case. He called his mother to tell her the interview had gone well, adding other news, that he had just made the dean's list. The Boiardis were unable to make it to Ithaca after the one-game postponement. "I tried to call him back," Deborah Boiardi says. "He was already off. I just said have a good game. I love you."

Next came the lacrosse game, a 4 p.m. start. The Big Red led Binghamton by three goals with two minutes and thirty-three seconds remaining. Binghamton had possession, and a starting attackman launched a shot toward the goal. Boiardi jumped in front of it and blocked it, thwarting the scoring opportunity. He took a few steps, then fell to the Schoellkopf Field turf. Trainers raced to attend to him; others nearby immediately called 911. Players from both teams knelt on the ground in prayer, light snow falling around them. Three minutes after the initial 911 call, at 5:49 p.m., emergency personnel from the Ithaca Fire Department arrived. LaFalce, providing analysis for the game on WHCU-AM, still remembers the horrifying sound of sirens drawing closer to the lacrosse field. Boiardi received advanced life support. He was placed in an ambulance at 6:05 p.m. and received further treatment. Ten minutes later, the ambulance left the field and took him to nearby Cayuga Medical Center. Players from both teams went into their locker rooms, visibly shaken and waiting for news. The remainder of the game was canceled. At the Cayuga Medical Center, at 6:44 p.m., Mario St. George Boiardi was pronounced dead. He was twenty-two years old. In the home team locker room at Schoellkopf Field, Tambroni delivered the news of Boiardi's death to devastated players and staff. They gathered again the next morning to meet with Boiardi's parents.

Boiardi's mother went to every player in the locker room, reassuring them, telling them how much her son loved them. "This is a lesson to make sure you spend time with your friends, love your family, and look out for others as well," she said, according to a 2016 *New York Times* article. "Tell your friends and family you love them." Later, when she retrieved her son's winter coat, she found in a pocket a slip of paper with Fr. Tim's phone number.

Cornell's next game, against the University of North Carolina in Chapel Hill, North Carolina, was canceled. The team took the bus trip anyway, just to leave Ithaca for a few days. On the way back they were part of the overflow crowd at Holy Trinity Catholic Church in Georgetown for Boiardi's funeral. That day, his father spoke publicly. "I don't fault any of the coaches, the players, the trainer, the university, or the equipment that he was wearing that day," Mario Boiardi said in a statement. "George was out there believing he was ready to play the game. That's all that matters." After several days, and with encouragement from the Boiardi family, Cornell decided to continue its season. Boiardi's locker remained untouched, and officials painted a white *21*, his jersey number, behind the goal closest to the team's locker room. Players added to their jerseys a patch with a hard hat and the number 21. The initial practices, understandably, were rusty. The Big Red won its first game back, 10–6, over Yale. Three days later, Boiardi family members joined players and coaches and more than eight hundred people in an overflow crowd at Cornell's Sage Chapel for a memorial service. Nine teammates and friends spoke. Other speakers included a professor in the American Indian Program who had taught Boiardi. Lloyd Elm had played lacrosse on the Onondaga Nation teams of the 1950s, once scoring three goals in a scrimmage against Hamilton College. A gifted student, he was sent to Haskell School in Kansas, then attended Emporia (Kansas) College for three years. Prior to his senior year, he returned to Central New York to be with his ailing father on the Onondaga reservation. With one year of eligibility remaining, he spent the spring of 1960 as a midfielder on the Syracuse lacrosse team, then earned an undergraduate degree from Syracuse and a grad school degree from Penn State.

In Elm's remarks at Sage Chapel, he said the Native American culture knows lacrosse as a medicine game, a game of healing. Boiardi "played a healing game," he said, "in a very beautiful way." Elm also presented Tambroni and the three captains a wooden lacrosse stick he made by hand. Elm made one request: "Put this in a place that will honor him." The players and Tambroni placed it in Boiardi's locker, where it remains to this day.

Cornell's season resumed with a 10–8 loss to Penn in Philadelphia. Tambroni wondered if the team was emotionally spent and exhausted. The players decided not to play for Boiardi, but to play as he would have done. "George wanted to be a teacher," one of them said in a video about Boiardi's life. "And he taught us a lesson on how to live day to day with respect, hard work and honesty." What lay ahead was a handful of Ivy League games that would make or break the season. A four-game stretch where Cornell needed to win all four for any chance at the NCAA tournament. Here, instead of trying to play for George, they decided to play like him, to be the best version of themselves every day, following the example of their team captain.

The first game was against Harvard on April 10 in Cambridge, Massachusetts. With less than four minutes to play, Cornell trailed by two goals. Junior Justin Redd assisted on a goal to close the deficit to one, then another Redd assist in the final minute tied the game at 8. In overtime, Redd fed freshman Brian Clayton for an open shot. Clayton scored for a 9–8 victory. The following week in Ithaca, the Big Red and Dartmouth were tied in the final seconds. Cornell generated a close shot; the Dartmouth goalie made the save. Overtime appeared certain. But the goalie did not control the rebound. The loose ball went to the prolific Greenhalgh, at the time in a shooting slump, fifteen goals in nine games. This time his shot was true. Cornell won, 12–11.

Princeton was the next Ivy contest. Tierney and the Tigers had won eight consecutive games in the series. As the Big Red disembarked from the team bus and entered Class of 1952 Stadium, an eerie fog enveloped the parking lot and playing field. In the same stadium where Boiardi decided to attend Cornell, the Big Red and Princeton played a classic. Cornell led by two in the final minutes, only for Princeton to tie the game and send it to overtime. The Big Red won the opening face-off, and Redd scored the winning goal in a 12–11 victory. Tambroni and DeLuca leaped over the fence separating the fans from the playing field to hug Deborah and Mario Boiardi. After the game, Redd raced out of the visiting locker room, even before taking a shower, and greeted the Boiardis. "George was here," he said to them. "We all felt it." The winning streak was three. One more was needed. In the conference finale in Ithaca, Cornell led Brown by one goal in the final seconds, though the Bears had possession. As they mounted a final attack, freshman goalkeeper Matt McMonagle from Philadelphia intercepted a pass to secure the 10–9 victory. Cornell's players stormed the field. In four must-win games, the Big Red won them, all by one goal. One player later said it felt as if the team had a guardian angel watching over it the whole time. The Big Red clinched a share of the conference title; with the tiebreaker, they earned an automatic berth in the NCAA tournament. "It's no coincidence," DeBlois told reporters, "that we bounced back from something so traumatic and we are pulling out one-goal games. It gets to that situation and there is no panic." Tambroni said after an early loss to Penn, he worried the team would have a tough season results-wise. "I didn't think they were in it emotionally," he told reporters. "They just found a way each and every week to dig in and draw on the courage of George."

Cornell's first-round NCAA opponent was Hobart. The winner would play the winner of the Penn-Navy game in the quarterfinal in Ithaca. Deborah and Mario Boiardi missed the game because they were visiting Red Cloud School with Fr. Tim. "George would have had a great time out there," Deborah says. "He always wanted to be a leader, and he always wanted to help other people. If someone felt challenged or was hurting, he'd always lend an ear." Amid their tour of Red Cloud, they also placed a call to hear the result of the lacrosse game: Cornell 11, Hobart 5.

One day later in Annapolis, Navy dispatched Penn, also by an 11–5 score. The Midshipmen entered the tournament as the number-two overall seed, enjoying their best season in decades. To reach the semifinals, Navy would have to beat Cornell in essentially a road game. "It doesn't matter where we're playing," Navy Coach Richie Meade said after the Penn victory. "Everybody has a cross to bear in the tournament. That's where the fight is, so that's where we'll go." In mid-May 2004, the War in Afghanistan was a little more than two years old, the War in Iraq roughly one year old. Thousands of American servicemen and servicewomen were in harm's way. Among them were many Navy lacrosse alums. The week of the Cornell quarterfinal, a Navy SEAL stationed overseas sent the team a flag that had flown over a US base in a major combat zone in Afghanistan. He also sent a note scrawled on the back of a wrapper of MRE rations wishing the team luck and saying he was following the results as best he could. Other notes and emails, expressing similar sentiments, often rushed or written near combat, came into Meade's office from around the world. Both teams were playing for something far greater than themselves.

Quarterfinal day, May 23, arrived warm and sunny in Ithaca. A crowd of nearly twelve thousand fans flocked to Schoellkopf Field for a doubleheader featuring, in the second game, Syracuse against Georgetown. Dozens and dozens of Cornell fans wore red T-shirts with Boiardi's 21 on the front and his name on the back and sat behind the team bench. The Big Red players took the field and formed a circle around the *21* painted behind the goal closest to the Schoellkopf locker rooms. Navy took the field next, led out by a player carrying the American flag sent by the Navy lacrosse alum now serving as a SEAL. Navy's coaches wanted an early lead, to keep the crowd quiet and not give Cornell confidence. Incredibly, just as at Princeton, a fog enveloped part of the playing surface, reaching the players' ankles in the early first quarter before dissipating. The first quarter ended scoreless, a rarity in lacrosse.

Early in the second quarter, Navy took its preferred early lead after sophomore Graham Gill scored the opening goal. Cornell briefly led 3–2 before Navy retook the lead. The Midshipmen led by a goal in the final minute when they were called for a penalty. Cornell's excellent and well-drilled extra-man unit took the field. The crowd rose to its feet in anticipation. An errant pass led to a scramble near the Cornell sideline. After a prolonged skirmish, Navy sophomore Steve Looney emerged with the ball and raced away from traffic. The Midshipmen held on, 6–5. Cornell's season was over. The Cornell fans in red gave a standing ovation. As the players left the field for the final time, an emotional and remarkable and unforgettable season completed, Tambroni walked within a few feet of Georgetown Coach Dave Urick, preparing his team for the second quarterfinal. Urick coached Tambroni at Hobart, and he took time from his team's preparation to hug his protege. "It's not the destination," Urick said into Tambroni's ear. "It's the journey."

Cornell's coaches later met to determine the winner of the Ray Van Orman Award, essentially the team MVP. The name is placed on a plaque near the Cornell lacrosse locker room. For 2004, there is one name: George Boiardi.

Cornell's seniors would appear on the turf at Schoellkopf Field one last time, roughly a week after the quarterfinal loss, for graduation. Boiardi was awarded a degree posthumously. His name was announced and cheered with every one of his teammates and classmates and friends. That night, there was a large gathering at a house near campus for the lacrosse players and coaches and families who had been through so much and grown so close. Deborah and Mario Boiardi gave each senior a graduation present, something they had once given their beloved son. It was a paperweight, white with black letters, and a quote from Ben Franklin: "Well done is better than well said."

George Boiardi's impact went beyond the 2004 season. His locker remains intact, with the stick from Professor Elm inside, along with a 2004 red 21 team jersey, a pair of lacrosse gloves, and a few of his team-related awards. Coach Connor Buczek acknowledges it can sound odd when he speaks of his relationship with Boiardi, given the two never met. Still, Buczek has his reasons. As a freshman in the spring of 2012, Buczek changed positions and found himself struggling for playing time. When Cornell played conference games on the road, Ivy League travel restrictions made it impossible to bring the entire roster. The limit on players for overnight trips was thirty-two. Buczek was outside this select group; for all three Ivy League regular season road games in 2012, he was left home.

Buczek spent the time shooting on the goals at Schoellkopf Field by himself, partly, he says now, to improve, partly also to clear his mind. He'd then sit in the locker room, late into the evening, all alone, staring at the locker of Boiardi, seeking inspiration as if he were lighting a votive candle and praying a novena. "I just felt I couldn't get the outcome I was chasing," Buczek says. "I was not sure which direction this was all headed. Those late nights at Schoellkopf, I was just trying to clear my head and get some direction. I needed to grab onto something, and that something was George and the legacy he left us. It was time to grab onto being a great teammate, to work hard, to care about the people around you, and to be present in every moment.... The relationship [with Boiardi] shapes a lot of guys, especially at their low points. It helps them find the narrative they're chasing."

That March 17 afternoon changed Cornell lacrosse. It is also spelled out by Tom Howley, the strength and conditioning coach. He began working with the team in the fall of the 1995–96 academic year, toward the end of Richie Moran's tenure, and worked closely with Boiardi. Though he officially is semiretired, he remains on staff for men's lacrosse. Howley's lineage is Moran to Pietramala to Tambroni to DeLuca to Kerwick to Milliman to Buczek. In October 2016 Howley released the book *Complete Conditioning for Lacrosse*, part of a series for several sports by Human Kinetics Publishing. "The gains made in training today," he wrote, "are an investment that can be withdrawn in the heat of battle on game day!" Howley dedicated the book to his wife, with an addendum honoring Boiardi.

George "will forever be associated with playing the game the way it was meant to be played—with intensity, passion, and dedication," he wrote. "Before that incident, the goal of the team was to attain *success*, what Coach Jeff Tambroni described as 'fulfilling your own mission.' After that tragic day, the program's emphasis shifted to striving for *significance* through investing in the lives of others."

Walker Wallace recalled entering Cornell's locker room the first day of his freshman year, in the 2020–21 academic year, and snapping a picture of Boiardi's locker preserved in the team's locker room. Years later the photo remains the background on Wallace's smartphone. In the summer of 2022, when the locker room underwent a renovation, Buczek and Stevens worried about telling the construction crew about the importance of Boiardi's locker and why it needed to remain untouched and very different from the ones being upgraded. The leader of the project was Tim DeBlois. In the fall of 1999, on a lacrosse recruiting trip to Princeton, he and Boiardi sat in Class of 1952 Stadium and dreamed of being there one day, wearing carnelian red, and winning a big game. "We were worried about his locker," Buczek says, "and George sent us one of his teammates." DeBlois held onto the locker for safekeeping and returned it in pristine condition once the work was finished. Supervising the work from the university was the leader of the facilities management team, Joe Solomon. This, too, was serendipitous—Solomon had been a reserve goalie at

Cornell in the late 1980s; he had played for Moran and was a member of the Onondaga Nation.

On the inside of the new locker room's double-doors feature is a giant *WD > WS*—well done is better than well said, borrowed from Boiardi. Underneath is the slogan, in Greek, *Exo tes thyras ouden*. It means "Out these doors, nothing," an old saying from the US Marines, Richie Moran's outfit before he became an educator and coach. Essentially, it is a call for the players to form a united front in all things. Players tap a red metal sign, heavily discolored from decades of use, that says, "I will give my all for Cornell today." There are other knowing nods to Boiardi and Eamon McEneaney, killed in the September 11 terror attacks. When the team lines up for stretches before games, if football lines are present, as they are on the FieldTurf surface at Schoellkopf Field, the captains lead the endeavor from the ten-yard line. Another group of teammates line up on the twenty-one-yard line. Ten and twenty-one were the jerseys of McEneaney and Boiardi. For years, during workouts in Schoellkopf, and in neutral-site locations where possible, the numbers ten and twenty-one were placed on the scoreboard under *home* and *visitors*. The video shown to the freshmen every fall about Boiardi, at about the point they are starting to feel overwhelmed, lasts twenty-one minutes.

Cornell even created a statistic to honor Boiardi. A tough groundball or winning the race to the endline on a shot to give the Big Red possession, for instance, or setting a good screen for a teammate to release a shot on goal—things that either go unmentioned in the box score or aren't given context there—earn the team a 21. Basically, it is a recognition of hustle plays. The "21" category is listed along with the other 10 or so team in-game goals: save better than 55 percent of shots, shoot better than 33 percent, clear the ball better than 85 percent, ride back better than 20 percent, win better than 55 percent of face-offs, or "restarts" in Cornell's terminology, and so on.

The metrics are tracked on a whiteboard on a game-by-game basis. It is not a deification as much as a way of life. Boiardi died blocking a shot to help his team in an early season game played before a few hundred people. He changed positions, without complaint, going from longstick midfield to the thankless shortstick version. Long before ride-hailing apps were invented, Boiardi was known to stuff his Jeep Cherokee full of teammates and friends needing a ride back from a night out in Ithaca. He was set to spend at least two years at a Jesuit school on a Native American reservation in South Dakota, teaching the financially less fortunate and spiritually gifted. He was the best of Cornell, and of Landon School, and of lacrosse. Why not try to follow his example? Deborah Boiardi says she and her family receive letters from far and wide, from people who have been inspired by *The Hard Hat*. There's an annual letter from the freshmen at a Division III program for whom the book is required reading. One year it was required reading for the team at Gonzaga College High School in the nation's capital, which annually plays Landon in a highly anticipated matchup. (Fr. Jim English, the Jesuit who co-officiated George Boiardi's funeral at Holy Trinity, had been Gonzaga's president in the 1970s, and for years Gonzaga sponsored a summer service trip for a handful of rising seniors to volunteer at Red Cloud School.)

Senior Duke Reeder, a reserve longstick midfielder, arrived at Cornell in the winter of 2023 after playing football for two years at Stanford. In those two years, he barely picked up a lacrosse stick. He arrived in Ithaca to find that Gavin Adler and others, rather than being threatened by another defender, were ready to show him the ropes and help the San Francisco native during the frigid outdoor workouts. "There was definitely a learning curve," Reeder says. "But those guys were really encouraging me." Reeder's time at Cornell, and his exposure to Boiardi, changed his career trajectory. As he drew closer to graduation in the spring of 2025, earning a degree as a government major, Reeder announced he was seeking to become a social science teacher and assistant football coach at Archbishop Riordan High in San Francisco. When asked why, he had a quick answer. "There was a guy named George," he'd say. "And even though I didn't know him, I feel like I did. He was going to become a teacher. And if it was good enough for him, it's more than good enough for me." In the middle of spring of 2025, Reeder received a note welcoming him to the faculty at Archbishop Riordan for the 2025–26 academic year.

6

SPRINT, NOT A MARATHON

On the first day of fall workouts in the 2024–25 academic year, Cornell's players and coaches listed their goals. These were kept on the top page of their binders that serve as a de facto playbook. There were less than a half dozen goals. The first: Win the national title. "We made it very clear from the very first day," said Chris Davis, a senior and top shortstick defender. "I remember that first meeting with Coach Buczek. There wasn't any 'maybe this' or 'maybe that.' We were going for a national title. We made sure everyone in the locker room was on board with that." Further down the list: Win the Ivy League tournament. Win the Ivy League regular season title. Win the groundball battle each game. Beat Penn State, a new addition, a reference to the humbling 20-9 defeat the previous year and the 10-6 defeat the year before that. The discussion also turned to George Boiardi, the realization that the 2025 season was twenty-one years after he died, and he wore jersey 21. "The first day of fall practice we talked about the '21' year," says senior Hugh Kelleher, a starting midfielder, "and doing something big for George."

By this point, strength and conditioning coach Tom Howley had met with the coaches to discuss their focus for the upcoming season. Some years, it's to improve strength or a little bit of quickness. Other years the team could use a little more toughness. For 2025, Buczek, and Stevens, assistants Paolo Ciferri and Max Tennant, and director of player performance Mark Wittink asked Howley to prepare the team to more readily handle the unpredictable nature of lacrosse. "Each team is unique," Howley says. "And their objectives are unique. We want to try to incorporate that right away. The games in March, and April, and May, we think about those in August and September." For the 2025 season, the talent largely was there. There was more than enough experience given the unusual aspect of having essentially two senior classes, thanks to the COVID-19-related eligibility rulings from the NCAA. And motivation was not expected to be an issue given how the 2024 season ended. The coaches met with the seniors, canvassing opinions on what they thought the fall should look like.

Sheehan, the college lacrosse coach's son, knew right away. "We were all in agreement things needed to be more intense," he says. "In the previous falls, they had patted us on the back a little too much. They knew we could handle a little more. We wanted them to make it difficult. At the time, it was nice to have a lighter fall, and the coaches telling us we're doing well. All of a sudden you're on your buddies' living room couch on Selection Sunday and you don't make the tournament, and it's not so nice anymore."

Howley's workouts took place at different times of day, sometimes early in the morning, sometimes at 4 in the afternoon, other times at 6 p.m. The itineraries for the workouts also changed. He scheduled Monday-Wednesday-Friday conditioning, then added a surprise Saturday morning weightlifting session. And within the workouts themselves, there was no set regimen. Some Mondays featured a lot of sprinting. Other Mondays featured longer distance runs or agility drills. Within the workouts, too, were changes. Howley broke the team into groups, then designated a leader for each. He gave the leader, and only the leader, very specific instructions—run up and back five times, turning to your left on the first three turnarounds, then once to your right, then finish with another turnaround to the left. The group leader relayed the instructions to his teammates. Once the workout began, Howley and the coaches would sporadically shout a different direction, a "left!" when it should be a right. The players were told to listen only to their group leader, not anyone else. "We were waking up with the mindset of, we're getting better today because we're going to play on Memorial Day," says Michael Bozzi, a senior shortstick defender. "The coaches and coach Howley didn't want anybody's head to get too big, especially since the season didn't start for another six or seven months. It was like, 'How can we keep these guys working hard, keep them somewhat humble, and keep them on their toes, adaptable and reactive?' That fall, they changed the routines constantly. We could never ease into it, never relax."

Says Howley, "The fall really was a little bit different. One of the things the coaching staff mentioned to me, they wanted to incorporate the team's ability to respond and react to sudden changes in circumstances. Training can get a little bit boring, can become rigid and predictable. We wanted to change things up every now and then. . . . Sometimes we did things A-B-C, other times B-A-C. It wasn't anything magical. We just wanted the players to absorb information quickly. And we wanted to give them a lot of instructions, just like in practice and games. A coach can give three or four cues [in a game], now you've got to remember them in a specific order. We thought, why not incorporate that in training?"

Buczek says the change was much needed. "We had fallen into a routine," he said. "We were really good at executing things that were routine. We were not as good at adapting and overcoming. Whether it was in the weight room or on the field, we wanted to keep guys guessing. Just attack what's in front of you. We definitely threw some change-ups in terms of the schedule. We wanted to keep an experienced team off-balance."

Buczek and Howley emphasized, again and again, being on the razor's edge. In college lacrosse the margins are so thin, one move, one off-field decision, one cheating on a diet, can send the game, or the season, either the correct way or the wrong way. Another element to the fall workouts was the ensemble approach. Freshmen were encouraged to call out an older player, even a senior, if the older player was not living up to the standard. Brian Luzzi, a junior and reserve midfielder for the 2025 season, recalled being a freshman and telling a junior he hadn't gone all the way to the endline on one conditioning drill. Another time, during weightlifting, Luzzi tapped an older player on the shoulder. You're not bringing the energy, he told the older player. You're not encouraging anyone. We're looking up to you. "Freshmen feel empowered to hold every single person accountable, even seniors," Luzzi says. "We don't have a hierarchy like most teams have." There are other rituals. The team keeps its locker room very clean. On every sprint, players start behind the white line, not on it, nor even cheating a little to be in front of it. "We pay attention to the small details," Luzzi says. "We always say the way you do one thing is the way you do everything."

The theme of uncertainty extended beyond workouts and practices. Davis sat out the fall while recovering from back surgery the previous April 1. Davis is from Essex Junction, Vermont, off the beaten path for most college coaches. "Coaches aren't coming to Vermont to see you," he told *The Burlington Free Press*. "You have to go see them." In the fall of 2019, as a junior at Essex High, he signed up for Prospect Day at Cornell. He was coming off a sophomore season in which he scored sixty points as a starting attackman. At 6-feet-3, 190 pounds, Davis also was a standout wide receiver. Players attending the prospect day were divided into two groups, those whom the Cornell coaches had seen and wanted to see again and those they did not know much, if anything, about. Davis was in the latter category. He went with the coaches assigned to his group, some from Ithaca College, a local Division III program. Most of the Cornell presence, including Buczek and Stevens, was on the other side of the field. During a water break, Stevens lightly asked one of the Ithaca coaches if anyone in his group showed promise. As Stevens recalls, the coach immediately said, "Yeah, that fucking kid," and pointed to Davis. When play resumed, Davis joined the group monitored by Stevens and Buczek. By the end of the day, Stevens collected Davis's contact information. Fearing word would spread on Cornell's hidden gem, it took about an hour for Stevens to express an interest in Davis via email. By this point, Davis and his family were headed back to Vermont. "The cell phone service on our ride home is awful," Davis says. "I tried to email coach Stevens and it didn't go through, I didn't have email service for two hours. Then I tried calling and I couldn't understand him, then he called and couldn't hear me. I was freaking out. I just thought it wouldn't work out." Eventually, technology cooperated. Davis committed to Cornell.

When he arrived for the 2021–22 academic year, he was quickly moved from attack to defensive midfield. He picked up the position change without complaint. Davis progressed enough to play a leading role on the team that reached the NCAA title game. He played every game as a sophomore in 2023 and scored goals against Lehigh and Army. As a junior in 2024 he injured his back in the blowout loss to Penn State. The surgery in April in Burlington, Vermont, was supposed to have healed his herniated discs. When Davis arrived for the fall of his senior year in 2024, he was still in a lot of pain. Bozzi, Davis's roommate in the house on East Seneca Street, recalled asking how his close friend was doing. "He'd say, 'I haven't slept in three days,'" Bozzi says. "He'd say it hurts to sit down, then hurts to stand up again. We had more of those types of conversations than we had positive ones." Soon, Davis was unable to sit through his classes. His parents scheduled another doctor's visit to the hospital in Burlington. If Davis needed a follow-up corrective surgery, his prospects of playing in 2025 were slim at best. Jarett Wait, Cornell alum and longtime supporter of the lacrosse program, recalled seeing Davis's father at a fall event. When describing his son's health, Gary Davis was near tears. Stevens, too, said he was planning a defense without its best shortstick defender.

The 2024 fall finished on the last weekend of October, with a scrimmage against Maryland in College Park. By all accounts, Cornell led 6–2 at halftime, at which point both teams began substituting players. Maryland goalkeeper Logan McNaney, star of the 2022 victory on Memorial Day, was coming back from an injury and played only in the third quarter. The fall scrimmage against outside competition signaled the formal end of the off-season period known as fallball. The messaging continued. Howley is well-respected enough that a less-than-stellar assessment from him can be a reason for crisis. "The players revere him," Wittink says. "One lukewarm assessment from him on a Friday morning after a lift, and you'll beat yourself up all weekend for not paying sufficient attention to detail and not having the right amount of energy. He never says something like, 'You suck.' It's not a direct confrontation. He'll just say yeah, that wasn't our best. And you know your beer is going to taste terrible all weekend."

In mid-November, Cornell announced its captains: Wallace, CJ Kirst, Bozzi, Davis, and Michael Long. Junior Charlie Box, a defensive midfielder, earned the hard hat, joining on the roster previous winners Kirst and Long. (Buczek also earned the hard hat in his junior year, 2014.) A few days later, technically after the fall season had completed, the seniors and fifth-year seniors met the coaches. The coaches conveyed a concern: The players were a little too satisfied with the fall performance. "Our coaches talked to us about where we think the team is, how everyone is doing," says Alex Holmes, a reserve midfielder. "They made it sound like we had a lot left to do. A lot of us thought we were in a good place. I remember the coaches being like, 'We disagree.' They thought we weren't where we needed to be, they called out the leadership."

On Tuesday, November 19, as the campus prepared for Thanksgiving break in around a week, the players met Howley for a late-afternoon workout. Junior Jack Cascadden, arguably the best face-off specialist in the nation and still recovering from knee surgery, missed the workout as he was taking an exam in his business computing class. Long and Kyle Smith also missed it; they were home for the fall semester, choosing to use their final semester of eligibility during the spring. A group of players dealing with or recovering from injury, including Hugh Kelleher and Walker Wallace, went to do their own workout on exercise bikes in the Schoellkopf Field field house. The rest of the team went to the Ramin Room, the indoor Astroturf facility. Howley set up mini-hurdles, roughly ankle high, for an agility drill. Anyone who knocked over a hurdle was to pick it up and start the drill again. The team broke into a half dozen groups. Howley blew his whistle. Players from almost every group kicked over a hurdle, then another, then still another. The drill restarted, only for the next player to kick a hurdle, restarting the drill yet again. Howley blew his whistle. He asked for greater attention to detail. The drill resumed. Again, hurdles went flying. After a couple minutes, Howley blew the whistle a third time. He told the team the attention to detail was not where it needed to be. The longstanding tradition was for the offending player or players to be kicked out of the workout while the rest of the team remained. This time, Howley dismissed the whole team. They were done for the day. "It was the first time any of us had seen coach Howley kick everyone out," says midfielder Andrew Dalton, a fifth-year senior. "We were pretty rattled."

The players formed their tight-two formation and began jogging back to the locker room. "You could hear it in his voice, we let Coach Howley down," Kirst says. "We let the coaches down. We let a day slip, and we couldn't let a day slip if we wanted to win the national title." On the run back, a few of the seniors bounced ideas off each other on how to respond. Then Kirst said, "Screw it, I've got it." He ran upstairs to the injured players on exercise bicycles. "I saw him and thought, wait, the workout is done already?" says Kelleher. "He just said, 'Come to the locker room. Now.'" There, a few seniors cleared the air. They called on their teammates to increase the effort and intensity, fast. Being kicked out of the workout by Howley was embarrassing. Kirst then said, almost thinking out loud, "I don't know about you guys, but I'm going to the field hockey field to do some conditioning. If we can't even make it through a workout, we'll never win a national championship. We're going to see who's in and who's not." Every player in the locker room, injured or not, stood up. They ran in tight-twos to the field hockey turf, next door to Schoellkopf Field, adjacent to the student parking lots. By this point it was dusk. Also by this point, Kirst had not figured out a course of action for what would happen once they arrived on the turf. "We all ran a 100-yard down-and-back, then a 50-yard down-and-back," Kirst says. "Then Duke Reeder says, 'That wasn't hard enough. We should do a 100-yard dash at a full sprint.'" Kirst agreed. He told the group, "We're doing it class by class, baby." Then began the call: Seniors, go! Juniors, go! Sophomores, go! Freshmen, go! With Kirst running as well. Kirst says he divided by class in the hopes individual leaders would take ownership. After a few sprints, Kirst told the group they hadn't done anything special in a Cornell jersey yet. "And we have to make this year special." Thus convened another round of class-by-class sprints. Because field hockey season had ended a few weeks earlier, the turf was free, but the stadium lights were not on. As most of the players ran sprints, the ones nursing injuries went to the sideline, doing push-ups or the isometric exercise known as planks. Kirst gave a "Go!" and the players sprinted 110 yards, from one end of the turf to the other. At the other end, they collected their breath, then Kirst lined them up and gave another "Go!" After the seventh or eighth sprint, starting goalkeeper Wyatt Knust began to ease up. "I thought we were about to finish," he says. Kirst gave another round of "Go!" and then another, then another. Their only light by this point was from a lone car in the parking lot; a student fiddling with their smartphone left their car headlights on. After fifteen or so sprints, the car pulled away, taking the remaining light with it.

 The players stayed on the turf, racing 110 yards. Back in the locker room was warmth and snacks and comfort and all-American certificates and red satin banners with white letters, in glass cases, for each of Cornell's NCAA tournament titles. They were from 1971, 1976, 1977. Back in the locker room was a forty-eight-year title drought. On the cold field hockey turf was a group of players wearing their Teagle T-shirts and shorts, surrounded by darkness, embarrassment, and the unknown. After several more sprints, a few juniors shouted encouragement. More sprints, and a couple sophomores spoke. Then more running, encouragement, running. Kirst says now he had formed a plan—they would run until Jayson Singer, the best on-ball defenseman on the team, the senior who turned down Virginia and Yale to win a national title at Cornell, addressed the group. Another break, more speeches, none from Singer. The sprints resumed. More speeches, nothing from Singer, more sprints.

The ordeal reached the two-hour mark. It was so dark players couldn't tell who was running next to them. They also lost count once the 110-yard sprints reached 40. Back in the Schoellkopf Field field house, the coaches and Howley mused on where the players had gone. "We can hear every time the locker room door opens and closes," says Stevens. "We know every time someone goes in there. I hadn't heard anything in a while, I just figured I'd missed it." Added Howley, "The team was not particularly focused that day. We tried to hold the seniors accountable for the performance of everyone. We said, 'This is your team. And they're not living up to the standard.'"

After forty-five sprints, after forty-five sets of planks and push-ups and sit-ups on the sideline, the running continued. One senior no one could see called out, "We love each and every one of you. Let's pick it up on this next rep." Then Kirst called "Go!" and they launched themselves forward, racing toward an endline 110 yards away and, perhaps, to destiny. After at least fifty sprints the players lined up for another. Seniors called out encouragement, reminding the team of the examples set by Boiardi and McEneaney, of the importance of being accountable. Then another sprint. After some trash talk from Kirst, Singer, not to be confused with the most loquacious member of the team, quickly addressed the group. "I wanted everyone to have a voice," Kirst says. "Every senior had to speak. Jay said a couple great words. Then we ran a few more sprints and gathered in a huddle. I not only saw how exhausted the guys were, but it was also a moment of a full group buy-in."

After this, after more than two hours in the cold and dark, Kirst called an end. The team formed its tight-twos and jogged back to the locker room. "What's crazy," says Holmes, "is I reached a certain point I had never been before. I had worked to my limit in workouts, but never past my limit. Not until that day. After a while my legs turned to jelly. Then I couldn't feel my legs. The funny thing is, once we got back in the locker room, I swear if someone had told me to go back out and run again, I could have done it. When you're with your teammates and all of you are uncomfortable but still encouraging each other, you can do anything." Sheehan said he later conducted an informal poll of Cornell lacrosse alums, going back at least fifteen years. None had ever seen nor heard of Howley kicking an entire team out of a workout. "There was a consensus that if we put ourselves through this, we'd be better off for it," Sheehan says. "It was one of the more powerful moments I've been part of." Added Luzzi, "It was terrible running that much. But the guy next to you was willing to get back on the line and run again, so you did it, too."

Most of the players took twenty or thirty minutes to muster the energy to take a shower. Sophomore Walker Schwartz, a longstick midfielder, did not have that luxury. He was due to take a business computing exam, the same one as Cascadden, but at a later time. The two ran into each other in the hallway outside class. "I asked him how the workout went and he said, 'We got kicked out and ran and ran,'" Cascadden says. "I was in disbelief. The look on his face, it looked like he had just come back from war. He said, 'I've got to get to my exam.' When I walked back to the locker room I didn't really know what to say." But he knew what to do. Running was not an option on his injured knee. The next morning Cascadden went to the stationary assault bicycles at Schoellkopf Field's field house and rattled off fifty-plus 110-yard sprints. Smith, back at his family's home in Sudbury, Massachusetts, spent November 19 working construction to stay in shape and earn some money. He quickly learned of the endless sprints on the field hockey turf. When asked if he felt lucky to miss it, Smith answers quickly. "Actually I'm sorry I missed it," he says. "I'm a little bit jealous. That was the moment everything clicked, and I wasn't there."

Almost immediately, the punishing workout took its toll. The day after, senior Rory Graham, an attackman and extra-man specialist, emerged with eight bags of ice on his sore body. A handful of others, including Sheehan, Reeder, and Dalton, suffered hamstring injuries, though none would be out long term. As the fall semester ended, Howley reiterated the razor's edge theme. He said lacrosse, and life, often plays out on a razor's edge. And it's important to be alert, to be ready, and to make sure you fall on the right side of the equation. Then he gave each player a plastic container for a single razor blade, with a rubber band around it, asking them to look at it daily and remember the message. Holmes, and others, kept it with them throughout the season. It appeared Cornell had been on the razor's edge of either being satisfied or being desperate for a title. Kirst had led them past the temptation of satisfaction and into terra incognita, well beyond their previously navigated limits.

7

MEDICINE GAME

Even when the lacrosse players are home over winter break, they still have conditioning work. Howley gives each player a list of workouts and exercises to complete. In a "trust but verify" moment, when the players come back to campus in January, they are given the "C Test" conditioning program, to see if they are in shape and ready for the season. In December and January, Sheehan and sophomore Luke Gilmartin, a shortstick defender, shoveled the snow in their Syracuse suburb and ran hills. They passed the C Test conditioning regimen, as did their teammates. All except Davis. He was exempted. On December 23, in his native Vermont, he underwent a corrective surgery on the herniated disc in his back. Doctors gave him an optimistic timetable of three months for when he could begin running. Davis remembers immediately looking at the Cornell schedule. March 23 was the week of the regular season game against Penn in Ithaca, about the halfway point of the regular season.

In Bernardsville, New Jersey, CJ Kirst and Mikey Long met for winter workouts. Long picked up Kirst, then drove to pass and shoot the ball at a field near Kirst's house, then went to the YMCA to lift weights, then grabbed burritos from a fast-food restaurant chain. Sometimes they did the drills twice in the same day, their own version of football's "two-a-days." During one of their shooting drills, Kirst complained of pain in his right hand. Long and his father helped Kirst schedule a doctor's appointment, though it is unclear if anything came from it.

Back on campus, in the preseason, Cornell's offense began its work on its 1-3-2 formation, a scheme predicated on passing, off-ball movement, setting picks, and looking for the player on the backside of the defense, or the area away from most of the defensive attention. The player usually is accessible via a skip pass and must shoot the ball quickly, before the defense becomes alert to the threat. Buczek wanted his players to be unselfish, to make the extra pass, literally passing up a good shot for an even better one, just as he referenced in the news conference after his final college game, the loss to Albany in the 2015 NCAA tournament. With Long back on campus for his final semester, he joined Kirst and sophomore Ryan Goldstein on the starting attack. Goldstein took over the quarterback spot, moving Long to the right-handed spot, with Kirst on the left. The first midfield was Sheehan, senior Hugh Kelleher, and lefty sophomore Willem Firth. Alex Holmes and Andrew Dalton anchored the second line, with sophomore Ryan Waldman and junior Brian Luzzi rotating in on the third spot. With the assembled talent, the key was not to overthink things. As Sheehan says, "Good lacrosse is simple lacrosse."

The defense featured senior Jayson Singer and juniors Brendan Staub and Matt Dooley. Here, too, the identities were clear. The Big Red prefers an aggressive man-to-man defense and sends its shortstick defenders very high up the field to meet the offensive midfielders as they enter play. Singer was the best on-ball defender, with the quickest feet, and would guard the top attackman. Staub was the physical presence, 6-feet-1, 210 pounds, likely to draw the best dodger. Staub also was arguably the smartest player on the team. He was a standout defensive end-linebacker at Garden City High on Long Island. His high school football coach told *Newsday* Staub was a once-in-a-lifetime player—and person. He scored in the ninety-ninth percentile in the ACT standardized test and, in the classroom, eclipsed the 100 percent barometer, essentially a 4.0 grade-point average. Staub also had motivation after how the 2023 season ended, the overtime loss to Michigan in the NCAA tournament when he was a freshman. Dooley was the best off-ball player, a high school all-American at Sudbury High outside Boston, and, at 6-feet-4, 200 pounds, an imposing presence. Dooley proved his chops in transition with the winning goal, with one second remaining, in the victory over Princeton the previous year, the game played on the twentieth anniversary of the death of Boiardi.

Senior Walker Wallace, a six-feet-six monster, improved to the point he was set to be the starting longstick midfielder. Walker Schwartz, a sophomore from Philadelphia with outstanding instincts going from defense to offense, was the second longstick midfielder. The main questions were the two areas targeted by Bill Tierney and his record seven NCAA titles—face-offs and goalkeeping. Knust was back after being in and out of the lineup the previous year. Also back was sophomore Matt Tully, who started the games after Knust was removed. And the coaches did not want a repeat of the on-again, off-again goalie dilemma. "Wyatt struggled at times, but we also mismanaged the goalie position by flipping back and forth" in 2024, defensive coordinator Jordan Stevens says. "We came into the year saying, Wyatt is really unflappable. He's not perfect, just like no goalies are perfect. But we knew what we'd get. He's a reliable presence. He's got nerves of steel, and a self-deprecating sense of humor to keep himself in check. He is what you want from a goalie at the highest level."

Face-offs were another matter. Cascadden had torn his ACL leading to the second game of 2024, and the Big Red never really recovered without him. Marc Psyllos, who played well in Cascadden's absence, had graduated. But Cascadden was a difference maker. At 6-feet-3, 220 pounds, a standout linebacker at Garden City (New York) High, he was a hot commodity on the recruiting circuit. Most college programs take only one face-off specialist each recruiting class. By September 3, 2020, his junior year, several specialists already committed. Cascadden narrowed his list to a handful of schools, including Cornell. He visited the campus in Ithaca during the COVID pandemic and hated it. "I wasn't allowed to meet any of the coaches or players," he says. "I drove around and really didn't like it. It felt like the middle of nowhere."

His mother is family friends with Dom Doria's family. She alerted Doria that her son's impression of Cornell was less than favorable, and he was considering a different Ivy League school. "We got on a call with Dom," Cascadden says, "and he told me about Cornell, he brought me around. After that I wanted to commit on the spot." Again, his mother advised caution. He should visit the rest of his schools. After his visits, Cascadden committed to Cornell. Now Cascadden was a junior and working his way back from his knee injury. As he recovered, junior Sam Ricci and freshman Michael Melkonian took the draws in practice.

Overall, the 2025 team was starting to look like another Richie Moran special. In 1971, Moran assembled a starting lineup including a defenseman who was a starting tight end on the football team and another who was a starting defensive lineman; an attackman who was the sixth man on the basketball team; another attackman who arrived on campus as a hockey recruit, having barely played outdoor lacrosse in his native Canada; and a goalkeeper who also played for Cornell's NCAA champion hockey team in 1970. (The two-sport goalie, the late Bob Rule, is believed to be the first person in history to win an NCAA title in two team sports.) With that lineup, and the thirty-four-year-old Moran running the show, Cornell won the inaugural NCAA tournament. Now the coach was Buczek, who wouldn't turn thirty-two until early June. And the roster included serious athletes. The Big Red featured the first four winners of the Tom Flatley Award, given to the top football-lacrosse player in Nassau County—Kelleher, Staub, Cascadden, and Melkonian. Not to mention senior Duke Reeder, the onetime Stanford outside linebacker who played on special teams as a freshman. And both Wallace and Singer, with one more year of eligibility—but in their eighth and final semester at Cornell—were putting out feelers to play Division I football.

After the interminable offseason, the unpredictable fall workouts, the hellish night on the field hockey turf, and the frigid early morning practices at Schoellkopf Field, the 2025 season finally arrived. The Big Red entered ranked number two in the USILA coaches' poll and number three in the *Inside Lacrosse* media poll. In both, two-time defending champion Notre Dame, with another strong team, was ranked number one. Cornell was set to open its season on February 15, against Lehigh in Bethlehem, Pennsylvania. First came two preseason scrimmages. The night before the first, against Marist in Ithaca, the team gathered for its pregame meal. The previous pregame spot, Italian restaurant Coltivare in the Ithaca Commons, closed in 2024. For the 2025 season, the Big Red splurged for night-before-the-game dinners at the on-campus Statler Hotel. There, the players, coaches, and staff enjoyed chicken parmesan with pasta and salad. Another tradition in the night-before meal is a senior speech. After everyone is done eating, a preselected senior addresses the team. He usually starts with a joke or funny anecdote before diving into wisdom or advice or platitudes he'd like to impart, especially to the younger players.

Because there were sixteen seniors, including the fifth-year group known as super seniors, the speeches began in the scrimmages and with Duke Reeder. In the days of early recruiting, Reeder spent the summer after his freshman and sophomore years at St. Ignatius Prep in San Francisco playing in recruiting tournaments. After his sophomore summer, believing he had done all he could to attract college coaches under the rules extant, he turned his attention to football, almost on a whim. "I had a bunch of friends on the team," he says. At 6-feet-4, 235 pounds, Reeder was a natural at linebacker and defensive end. He committed to Cornell for lacrosse until after his senior football season, when Stanford football offered him a spot as a preferred walk-on. He called Buczek and Stevens and told them he was decommitting. "They said, we can't fault you for this," Reeder says. "Good luck, and please let us know if anything changes." In late fall 2022, things changed. Reeder was playing sparingly on special teams, and Stanford was not exactly winning many football games—in 2022, his sophomore year, the Cardinal went 3–9. The thought of lacrosse kept nudging at him. Reeder reapplied to Cornell as a transfer, was accepted for the spring 2023 semester, and arrived in time for the coldest workouts of the year. He scored a goal in a scrimmage against Bucknell, otherwise playing as a reserve. In his senior speech, he recalled his first phone call home after arriving in Ithaca. "I called home, and it was, 'Tell me everything,'" Reeder says. "And I said, 'I really can't tell you about it. You have to be here to feel it and experience it. You feel an energy in all the things you do. It's really, really cool.'"

The second senior speech came the night before scrimmages against LeMoyne and Rochester Institute of Technology, a Division III power. After the meal at the Statler Hotel, midfielder Alex Holmes broke his remarks into three parts. One, he said, do not stress out about things that are out of your control. "What's done is done," Holmes said. "You can't change what's in the past." Two, smile. Always. "I got that from [former attackman] Monty Cook," Holmes says. "Smile every day in practice, smile even in difficult times. Positive energy is infectious." And three, when faced with a difficult decision, when debating between two courses of action, ask yourself what George Boiardi would do. "I said, if you do what you think George would do," Holmes says, "you'll find yourself on the right side of it at least 98 percent of the time."

After the preseason scrimmages, the regular season began with the opener against Lehigh. Cornell arrived at the Renaissance Allentown Hotel the night before the game. That morning, the forecast called for one to three inches of snow, with sleet and freezing rain. Lehigh moved the game up an hour, to an 11 a.m. start. To accommodate, Cornell left its hotel earlier than usual. Kirst spent time at Lehigh, as two of his older brothers went there. He immediately knew the bus was going the wrong way. "We passed a sandwich shop where I'd gone with my brothers," he says. "I remember thinking, this isn't the way to the stadium." The satellite navigation system suggested a route that, in the terrible weather, was impassable for the large team bus. To reach the Ulrich Sports Complex, Cornell had to drive all the way around Bethlehem, sticking to main roads. The Big Red arrived a little after 11 a.m., the moved-up start time. The complex does not offer locker rooms for visiting teams, so Cornell changed in an off-site location, further delaying the start. Buczek then asked for a near-complete warmup time of sixty minutes. "There are certain things you can't overcome," Buczek says. "We had been preparing all offseason for it, then it arrived in Week One." The game began at 12:03 p.m. With the assembled talent on offense, and especially the all-star attack, the first goal of the 2025 season came from sophomore Luke Gilmartin, a short-stick defender. He took a pass in transition from Long and scored on a rocket, low-to-low, taking the shot with a windmill-like release. The sequence underscored one of Cornell's strengths: A good shot is a good shot, no matter if it's from a starter or reserve. "CJ and Mikey Long instilled trust in you," says Luzzi. "They were two amazing players, and they used to tell me to shoot more. They trusted me to shoot. It was a big thing for them, that they trusted everyone on our team to shoot. It wasn't just, 'Give the ball to 15 [Kirst's jersey number] every play.'" Through the first three quarters, Cornell scored sixteen goals on thirty-eight shots (42 percent) and cruised to an 18–10 victory. Kirst finished with six goals, and sophomore Willem Firth added four. After the game, on the bus ride back to Ithaca, with roads slick and rain and snow falling, Kirst sat toward the back, reserved for the seniors, with Kelleher and Sheehan. "Lehigh is always a good test for us," Kirst says. "And you could start seeing our offense click as a group. All six of us were moving the ball and getting on the scoreboard. The defense followed the game plan. Everything was working. We sat there and said, holy cow, we have a really special group."

The second game, a week later, came against Denver. Two nights before the February 22 contest came the title game of the NHL's riveting 4 Nations Face-Off tournament. The final pitted the United States against Canada. It also pitted a couple Cornell lacrosse players against a couple coaches. Seniors Andrew Dalton and Rory Graham grew up in Toronto. Their experiences with lacrosse were mixed. Dalton, as a sixth grader, was cut from his team at Kingsway College. He played briefly for a club team before moving on to baseball. In grade nine, in the fall of the 2015–16 academic year, he enrolled at St. Michael's College outside Toronto. On the first day of school, in the first period of the day, he and Graham had the same English class, then moved to the same homeroom. They became fast friends. Soon, Dalton and Graham joined a friend group comprised largely of lacrosse players. Dalton decided to give the sport another try. Graham, too, had kept lacrosse largely on the back burner. His father had spent three seasons in the early 1980s in the NHL; Pat Graham played for Pittsburgh and Toronto before severe back pain ended his career. The elder Graham moved back to Toronto and became a chiropractor. Rory Graham grew up playing hockey and lacrosse. "I enjoyed hockey more," he says. "But I was a little better at lacrosse. . . . And I much preferred box lacrosse to field lacrosse. Growing up, I really didn't like the outdoor game at all." In Canada's grade nine, Graham and Dalton played on St. Michael's junior varsity team.

By grade ten, Graham progressed to varsity; Dalton remained on JV. In grade eleven, both were standouts on one of the top outdoor teams in Canada and drew attention from a number of schools, in part because they were planning to take a postgraduate year to help their development. One autumn Friday at St. Michael's, the pair excitedly talked between classes about going on college recruiting visits that weekend. They departed school, wishing each other luck and promising to compare notes on Monday. The next day, Graham and his family pulled up to Cornell, Graham wearing khakis and a polo shirt to meet the coaches and players. As they walked toward Schoellkopf Field, they saw Dalton getting out of his family car, wearing gym shorts and a workout T-shirt and carrying an empty fast-food bag. "We had no idea we were visiting the same school," Graham says. They both committed to Cornell.

Now they were seniors, and very proud Canadians, and very much among the more ardent hockey fans on the lacrosse team. They made a bet with Stevens and assistant coach Max Tennant. If the United States won the 4 Nations final, Dalton and Graham would tape their lacrosse sticks with American flag tape for the rest of the season. If Canada won, Stevens and Tennant had to wear neckties with the Canadian flag to every team event for the rest of the year. Graham, Dalton, and the super seniors gathered to watch the hockey game at their house on North Quarry Street. Canada won in overtime. Kelleher, a housemate slated to give his senior speech the next night, paid particular attention to the postgame interview from Connor McDavid, who had assisted on the winning goal.

The next night at the Statler, with Stevens and Tennant wearing red-and-white ties with a giant red maple leaf in the middle, Kelleher addressed the team. He began with a nod to Dalton and Graham. "You guys might like this one," he said. Kelleher then launched into something he had heard McDavid say in his postgame interview. "I mainly talked about the importance of confidence," Kelleher says. "Even Connor McDavid was talking about not having a good game [in the 4 Nations final] and struggling with his confidence before he made the game-winning assist. He said he was struggling the entire game but kept working his butt off. It was bad play after bad play, then in overtime he gets the big assist. I mean, the best hockey player in the world struggles with confidence." Kelleher made the somewhat surprising admission that he, too, struggled with his confidence, despite being a four-year starter and one of the top midfielders in the nation. "It's so important to stay confident," he said. "I struggle with it, too. Bad shots, shots I don't take. . . . Just manage the ups and downs. Keep trying your hardest and play with the same belief all the time." The next day against Denver, the opening goal came from Kelleher. Cornell led 11–3 midway through the third quarter when the second midfield entered. Holmes, while trying to make a change-of-direction cut, heard a snap, then fell to the turf. The son of an orthopedic surgeon, he knew right away it was bad. He was right. Holmes had torn his ACL and meniscus. "It was just a right-to-left split dodge," he said. "I've made that cut fifty thousand times. . . . I felt like I was the best player I'd ever been. The best shape I've been in. Just really bad luck." Holmes, who two weeks earlier encouraged the team to be positive in the face of all evidence to the contrary, now found himself taking his own advice. Cornell won, 15–5, with Kirst again scoring six goals. Holmes's injury muted the postgame celebrations.

In the third game, midweek against Hobart in Geneva, New York, Cornell fell behind 7–3. It then scored ten consecutive goals and cruised to a 22–7 victory. Kirst, for the third straight game, scored six goals. Next Cornell survived a long bus trip to Virginia and a determined Richmond team in a 12–11 victory to start the season 4–0. "We were living on the razor's edge," Kelleher says. "Richmond had out-toughed us in the middle of the field. Everyone was aware of how we were playing. And it was not up to our standard." This was true of Kirst as well. Earlier in the week he had complained to trainer Danielle Hemly of pain in his right wrist when he shot the ball in practice, similar to the pain he felt in the off-season workouts with Long. For the Richmond game, he asked for tighter tape on his wrist. He finished with three goals, breaking his streak of scoring six in every game.

Up next was Penn State in Ithaca. Beating the Nittany Lions was a team goal. Moreover, Penn State was without senior Matt Traynor, by far its most dangerous offensive weapon; he missed the game with an injury. With three minutes to play, Cornell led 12–8. Then Penn State scored to close the deficit to 12–9, with little more than two minutes to play. On the ensuing face-off, Cascadden, returning to game shape, and wearing a heavy brace on his left knee, scrambled for a loose ball when he delivered a crunching hit to a Penn State player. The referees blew their whistle to stop play. Cascadden was called for a penalty. The referees wanted a video review of the hit, to see if Cascadden made helmet-to-helmet contact. After watching the replays, they ruled he had done so. Cascadden was called for unnecessary roughness, the more severe two-minute version. The penalty was nonreleasable. The Nittany Lions scored, closing the deficit to 12–10. With Cascadden out, Melkonian assumed face-off responsibilities. He lost the ensuing face-off, and the Nittany Lions scored again to close to 12–11 with 1:18 to play. Melkonian won the next face-off; Cornell controlled the ball and called a time-out as the players on Cornell's sideline raced onto the field in celebration. When play resumed, Kirst started with possession, facing a double team. After about ten seconds he was pushed out of bounds, giving Penn State the ball. On the ensuing possession, with seventeen seconds remaining, Penn State tied the game. The teams traded possessions in overtime before senior Ethan Long scored the winning goal in Penn State's 13–12 victory.

In mere minutes, Cornell's undefeated season and a major team goal were gone. "Traynor is their quarterback," says Howard Borkan, a Cornell alum and former college coach. "And one of the worst things, and I know this as a New York Jets fan, is when the other team's starting quarterback is hurt. There isn't a lot of prep for the backup. You just don't know what the backup can do. I think that was the situation with Penn State and Traynor. Also, there is so much talent on these teams now. Guys sitting on the bench at the top programs, they are really good. They're just waiting their turn."

The previous year, Cornell lost a handful of one-goal games and missed the NCAA tournament. The 2025 season was mere weeks old, and Cornell had just lost another one-goal game. Cornell's coaches later said when the team was ahead 12–8, nearly a dozen things had to go wrong to lose the game. All of them did. "I just remember being almost in shock," says Wallace. "At no point did I feel like we were going to lose the game. . . . I don't think we were as dialed-in as we needed, and we kind of got exposed in that moment. The locker room was as silent as a locker room gets. That woke us up. And it probably scared us a little, too. Also because of our record against Penn State." The focus fell on Cascadden. Kelleher remembers giving him a pat on the back. Others joined in. "Jack, that's not on you. We win as a team and we lose as a team," Kelleher said, also reflecting on Melkonian's sudden introduction to the spotlight of major college lacrosse. "I actually wasn't sure who I felt worse for, Jack or Michael Melkonian."

Cascadden sat at his locker for a long time, going over the play leading to the penalty. "I remember the groundball popped out in front of me," he said. "I tried to go down and get it and got called for a two-minute penalty, which didn't really help us out. Penn State made play after play. Michael Melkonian did an unbelievable job to win a face-off, then we lost the ball. . . . I remember after that game it felt like we had lost the national championship, except the stakes weren't so high. There wasn't a word said in the locker room." When it was time to speak, Buczek reiterated the importance of finishing games off. "He talked to us a lot about that," Bozzi says now. "Finish, finish, finish." Long after the game ended, Tom LaFalce left the press box after providing analysis for the ESPN+ online broadcast. It was his youngest son's birthday, and his son had brought a group of friends to the game. They were running around the field. LaFalce was walking to meet them when something caught his eye. He saw Cascadden with his lacrosse stick throwing and catching a ball against the brick outer locker room wall, again and again and again. "You could tell he was pissed off," LaFalce says. "He looked so frustrated. I could almost feel him saying, 'I'm not letting that happen again.'"

Up next, on Saturday, March 15 in Ithaca, was the Ivy League opener against Princeton. The Tigers entered ranked number 2 in the nation, with impressive victories over Penn State, Duke, and North Carolina. Princeton also was ranked number one in the Ratings Percentage Index (RPI), a metric used in the NCAA tournament selection process. Before Monday's practice, Wallace spoke to the team about the importance of the week ahead and how the team's goals were on the razor's edge, just as Howley and Buczek always said. A good week would right the ship. "We came back," says Dalton, "with a heightened sense of urgency." In the locker room before practice, Cascadden began seriously thinking about ditching his bulky knee brace and switching to a smaller, sleeker compression sleeve.

On the field, drills began. Kirst felt more pain in his right hand. During a simple passing and shooting drill, he was barely able to catch the ball, then shot with only his left hand. He tried again, with the same result. His right hand wouldn't grip the lacrosse stick. Kirst ran off the field and sought out trainers Hemly and Ed Kelly. He asked Hemly for a tighter tape job on his right hand and wrist and rejoined practice. During a transition drill, his wrist gave out. He asked Graham, the backup lefty attackman, to take his place. The best player in lacrosse, with his 188 career goals, three short of tying Mike French's program record, raced toward the locker room. The injury that initially appeared over winter break was back and much worse. "I said my hand is killing me," Kirst says. "My head was spinning."

He asked a teammate, sitting out practice nursing an injury, to grab Kirst's wrist brace from the locker room. Kirst tried on the brace and still couldn't grip his lacrosse stick with both hands. Only his dominant left. He went home and iced his right hand and wrist. The next morning, it was still painful. Kirst and Kelly drove an hour for an MRI exam. Kirst says he remembers thinking many thoughts—his Cornell career might be over, he might need season-ending surgery. He also reflected on the loss of his father, Kyle, who had died suddenly in June 2015 at the age of forty-seven. A longtime lacrosse player, coach, and enthusiast, he encouraged his sons, and everyone with whom he came into contact, to play the game with a smile and with respect. In this moment, Kirst says, he saw Kelly as a father figure, though smiles were in short supply. The MRI confirmed the news: On March 13, 2025, Kirst learned he had broken his right hand.

When Kirst arrived on campus, he immediately went to meet with Buczek and assistants Stevens, Paolo Ciferri, and Griffin Buczek, Connor's brother. Kirst says now he was near tears. (Older brother Connor Kirst was a little more circumspect. Upon learning of the injury, he texted CJ back: "You've got a left hand, you'll be able to play.") Kirst went through his options. He could not grip a lacrosse stick. He also said he could not undergo surgery and be out at least five weeks, with a return at best in late April, by which point the Big Red might be in the same boat as the previous year, on the outside of the NCAA tournament. Connor Buczek looked him in the eye. "To hear him say, 'Hey, you're going to get through this,'" Kirst says now, "that confidence in his voice when I was on the verge of tears really calmed me down." Kirst went to the dining hall. Normally the team sits downstairs. Kirst, wanting to be alone, not yet ready to reveal his prognosis, ate upstairs, using only his left hand. He texted Long, finally telling a teammate the news, asking him not to share it yet. His close friend and teammate since their days with the Delbarton School Green Wave raced upstairs in the dining hall and gave Kirst more reassurance. "We'll figure this out," Kirst remembers his friend telling him. For the remainder of the practice sessions that week, Graham took over the lefty spot on attack, and Kirst was in the locker room, trying on any number of hard casts and soft casts and tape jobs and padding inside his right glove. What the trainers and Kirst settled on was a cast made almost of PVC pipe material. "I think he went to every doctor in Ithaca," says Kelleher. "When he got hurt the week of the Princeton game, everything on the field stopped." Kirst also adjusted the heavy tape at the bottom of his stick, known as a donut.

He readjusted it, then adjusted it again, finally settling on something that would keep his right hand in place.

As luck would have it, Kirst was scheduled to give his senior speech at the Statler on Friday, the night before the Princeton game. His remarks included making reference to his condition. "I basically just shared my journey," he says now. "And my thought process going forward. I was ready to give it my all. I had the opportunity to get surgery and not play, and I wasn't going to do that. I knew even if I wasn't scoring, I was just trying to find a way to help."

The next morning, as Cornell took the field in its tight-twos for pregame warm-ups, Kirst was nowhere to be seen. He was still in the locker room. Trainers and a local doctor were insisting he not play. Kirst pushed back. The two-time team captain and 2023 hard hat recipient would have surgery only if he was re-reinjured during the season, or after the season, whenever that was. Kirst would navigate periods of intense pain and a significant risk of reinjury. A doctor would be present on Cornell's sideline at every game, just in case his hand injury grew worse. Kirst also had to adjust to playing with a cast under his right glove, at a part of the season with little to no runway for such adjustments. It would be done on the fly. If he found himself face-guarded by the opposition, as Teat had been in the NCAA tournament in 2018, the Big Red was far better equipped to play five-on-five. They had seen the tactic before and were ready. In some ways, face-guarding would benefit Kirst, as it would mitigate a further injury. Those plans were up to the opponents. Kirst was only concerned with helping Cornell. When the Big Red reemerged from the locker room in its tight-twos minutes before the opening face-off, Kirst and Wallace led from the front.

Andy Phillips, Cornell lacrosse alum, head of the Cornell Lacrosse Association, received a call while driving from his home in Manhasset, New York, to Ithaca the morning of the Princeton game. "One of the parents said CJ was a game-time decision," Phillips says. "It was described as not the kind of injury you play through, except that he did. The parent started describing the injury and I thought, 'Oh boy, I'm not sure I want to hear this.' It sounded bad. . . . In this day and age of training staff protocols on injuries, they're there to prevent players from being abused. Basically, CJ had to overrule everybody. He said, 'I'm playing.'" Added senior Michael Bozzi, a top shortstick defender, "There was a zero percent chance CJ was going to pull himself out of playing. His heart is a lot more powerful than his actual body." In the opening minutes, Kirst threw a right-handed pass to Goldstein, who scored on a close shot. Kirst also scored on his first shot, a left-handed finish off an assist from Cascadden. Cornell won, 15–10, and Kirst finished with 5 goals, giving him 193 in his career, eclipsing the mark of 191 set by Mike French from 1974 to 1976. French was in attendance and, after the game, was pictured giving both Kirst and Kirst's mother a hug. Even the weather cooperated. The game was played in around sixty-degree temperatures, with many in the stands wearing T-shirts or light jackets. French told Terry Foy from *Inside Lacrosse* his thoughts on losing his career goals record at Cornell. "If I was to pick anybody in the world [to break my record], it would be him," French said, "because he's a wonderful young man. He comes from a great family. . . . He's one of the best players I've seen in ages."

By this point, the coaches and staff were adjusting to Kirst's insistence that he play as long as possible before surgery. When asked if he initially thought the injury would end Kirst's season and likely his Cornell career, Buczek gave a quick answer. "At a certain point and time that was on the table," Buczek says. "For us, it took some time to figure that piece out. We were very fortunate. He didn't practice a ton in the middle of the season. Rory Graham was playing that role in practice. Rory didn't see all the results on the field, but he was a really important leader for us. Also Coach Howley. He put CJ through workouts [during practice], making sure he was prepared physically and mentally, almost mimicking the week we had of practice, but doing it on the sideline." Graham, for his part, said the first two days when Kirst missed practice were nerve wracking. "I didn't know the full extent of it," he says. "I was his backup and suddenly running with the first team. CJ is an impossible guy to replace, so I was pretty nervous. Plus I'd never started a game. I mean, I would have done fine. But the whole team was hoping he'd be able to play. That's not a knock on myself. It's a credit to how amazing he is. That [Princeton] game, he was Superman, and he continued to be the rest of the year." The following Saturday against Yale in New Haven, Connecticut, Kirst again insisted on playing. By this point, word had spread into a tight circle of Cornell supporters of the injury. Mike Levine, Big Red attackman in the early 1990s, was in the parking lot at Yale with a few other Cornell lacrosse alums on the morning of March 22 when Tim Goldstein relayed the news. "I remember I just had this sinking feeling," Levine says. "Once again, we had everything lined up and now it's not going to happen. And then Timmy said, 'I don't know, I think he's going to play.'" Kirst did more than play. He scored the game's first, second, third, ninth, and eleventh goals, all in the first quarter. By halftime he scored eight goals. He finished the game with nine goals and a still-broken right hand.

By this point, there was a growing number of fans in the Cornell cheering section. And many of them took their seats sporting little artistic concoctions pinned to their outwear. The provider was the so-called Button Lady. Her pins were homemade, a circle with a clear, hard plastic casing and the slogan for the week. They started simple, half red and half white, with "Beat Denver" and then "Beat Penn State." For the Ivy League opener, and seeing more people requesting and wearing her handiwork, Karen Lohnes dipped into her creativity. For the

Princeton game she depicted a Cornell bear standing at a stove front with the words "You like the heat? Welcome to our kitchen!"

In real life, Lohnes is the mother of sophomore Ike Lohnes, a reserve defenseman from St. Albans School in the nation's capital. She is a tax expert at one of the world's largest accounting firms, a summa cum laude graduate of Boston University Law School, married and the mother of three boys. She did her undergrad at LSU, in her home state. And home football games in the Southeastern Conference take on a life of their own. This includes the so-called spirit pins with a catchy slogan, or maybe it's kitschy, for home games and a postseason bowl game. (The service academies still create spirit pins for home football games, with slogans like "Abuse Syracuse!" and "Level Lehigh!" The midshipmen or cadets wear the spirit buttons on their dress uniforms at the stadium and often gift them to children who ask.) When Ike Lohnes, her oldest son, arrived at Cornell in the 2023–24 academic year, Karen went to the bookstore and politely inquired about spirit pins for the upcoming football game. "They didn't know what I was talking about," she says. "The LSU bookstore sells pins going back a while. At Cornell, I guess it isn't really a thing anymore. I decided to start making them." She began in the 2024 lacrosse season, with a run of about fifty pins per game. As the 2025 season showed promise, and both the enthusiasm for and importance of the games increased, Lohnes extended her run to 150. She makes them by hand, designing them herself, then breaking out her button-making machine and hard-pressing the design into clear hard-plastic shells with clasps on the back. Sometimes she gets a head start by making a batch in the fall, while watching Sunday NFL games.

For the Cornell-Yale game in New Haven—where Kirst scored eight goals in the first half, causing an excited Mike French to jokingly tell a friend, "Maybe they should break his other hand!"—Lohnes's button depicted a set of sharp teeth around the phrase "Take a bite out of the Bulldogs!" It was midseason, and Lohnes learned the idiosyncrasies of her adoring, albeit superstitious public. Some people can only receive the button in their right hand; others, only their left. Some need the pin right away, as soon as they see her. Others have to wait until they are about to enter the stadium. The pins are part of the collaboration among parents for each Cornell lacrosse game. In 2025, a group of parents created specialty cocktails, easily transferable into nonalcoholic mocktails, for many of the pregame tailgate parties. With an eye toward the early season games, often played in teeth-chattering cold, the parents concocted an Irish Good Luck Coffee, with coffee, whiskey, and freshly made whipped cream. Lohnes packs a blender in her suitcase and brings it to the tailgate, to get the whipped cream frothy and peaked just right. Because the Richmond game was played in mid-March and proved to be the team's farthest jaunt South, the parents concocted a Big Red Hurricane, in honor of upcoming Mardi Gras. Lohnes's pin for Richmond reflected her

Louisiana roots: "Lets Geaux Red." "There are so many ways we all try to get involved and have fun with it," Lohnes says, "and show support for the boys. They obviously put a ton of work into lacrosse, so we try to do things, too."

The pregame tailgates often featured food from Joe Lizzio, the face-off specialist and a reserve midfielder on the 1987 and 1988 NCAA runners-up. He kept a large grill in a shed near the Crescent Lot. On any given gameday he is liable to make a vat of his signature sausage and peppers and onions in tomato sauce. He also made his pièce de résistance, the Rocky Burger, made with three kinds of meat. Lizzio broke out the Rocky Burger toward the end of 2024 in a game Cornell lost. He brought the burger out again for the Penn State game in March, another loss. At this, Lizzio put it on hiatus until 2026, though he still makes them for Ryan Goldstein, as they are a staple of his diet on a gameday weekend. While Lizzio works the grill, he sends out parents and friends to tell people the food is for everyone, not just a select few. Among his hawkers are Timmy and Tommy Goldstein, Ryan's cousins; Mark Tully, the father of reserve goalkeeper Matty and a former Drug Enforcement Agency group supervisor in the Boston area; Alex Nikolic, father of injured midfielder AJ Nikolic and a former Cornell hockey player; and Todd Adler, a lacrosse alum from the 1990s and a very good chef. "They push product," Lizzio says. "People need to know this is for everyone. I don't care if we feed five hundred people or five people. As long as we're blasting music and eating good food, that's all that matters. . . . Show up to the grill and you get fed. Those are the rules."

In the week leading to the home game against Penn on March 29, two major events took place. One, Cornell's victories over Princeton and Yale were so impressive it entered the week ranked number one in the nation. It was Cornell's first time atop the polls since 2007. Second, this was the week Davis targeted to be cleared to return to practice, following his second significant back surgery in less than twelve months. Prior to the first surgery, his symptoms included sciatica, a pain that radiates down the back of the leg, often into the foot or toes; back pain, especially when sitting or standing for long periods; and difficulty walking or standing, let alone running and playing Division I lacrosse at its highest level. Davis confided in a few people, including Stevens, that for months at a time he could not feel his legs. The pain became so great he struggled to sit through his classes; he majored in communications and minored in business, making the honor roll along the way.

Coming back from one major back surgery in less than a year was tough enough. Davis was trying to come back from two. "To say his back surgeries were significant is an understatement," Stevens says. "We were under the impression after the [2024] Penn State game he'd never play again." His teammates were under the same impression. "The short version is no, I didn't think there was a chance he'd play again," says Graham. "There were times even he said he was done. He was still showing up, still doing everything he could do. He kept a really strict diet. He basically did everything right." On March 25, a Tuesday, Davis walked slowly onto practice at Schoellkopf Field. He was back, cleared for light drills, eyeing a return for the Albany game on April 1. That day was exactly one year since his first surgery, when he lay in a hospital bed in Burlington, Vermont, far away from his teammates and coaches and friends, wondering if he'd ever play the sport again. Now the best shortstick defender for the top-ranked team in the nation, seeking to end a forty-eight-year title drought, was set to begin his final season. Stevens remembers watching Davis begin a drill. The coach then turned around and pretended to look at something at the other end of the stadium. He later said he was simply trying to hide the tears in his eyes.

On Saturday, March 29, Penn entered Schoellkopf Field with the two main foils from the previous year's Ivy League tournament back on the roster. Senior goalkeeper Emmet Carroll, who made nineteen saves that night, was in goal, alongside his high school teammate and childhood friend, senior Brendan Lavelle, one of the best defensemen in the Ivy League set to guard Kirst again. Cascadden took the opening face-off wearing a lighter, sleeker compression sleeve on his knee. He instantly looked more mobile. "I came to the conclusion the concerns about my knee were holding me back," he says. "It was selfish on my part. When the brace came off, I felt much more explosive. I felt so much faster." Cascadden won the first five face-offs. By the middle of the first quarter, the Big Red had goals from its first midfield (Firth), its second midfield (sophomore Ryan Waldman), its starting attack (Long), and its extra-man unit (Kelleher, assisted by Kirst). The 4–0 lead became 10–1 at halftime. Early in the third quarter it ballooned to 12–1. The Big Red won, 15–5. Cascadden won twelve of nineteen face-offs and added eight groundballs.

The night before the midweek Albany game on April 1, at the Statler Hotel, Danny Caddigan gave his senior speech. "I wasn't a guy who was all over the stat sheet," he says of his remarks. "It didn't matter. I was so happy to be with this team, and this group of guys. That's what I told them. These guys are my best friends, and will be forever. I just wanted to be remembered as a guy anyone could come to, whether they needed a laugh or a hug." The next day, at Schoellkopf Field, Bozzi took the first face-off wing as shortstick defender. Junior Charlie Box took the second. Less than three minutes into the contest, Davis stepped onto the field, in tandem with sophomore Luke Gilmartin. The previous year, the shortstick defender spot was Cornell's major weakness. Because of injuries, the Big Red had to move senior Aiden Blake, an offensive midfielder, scorer of crucial goals down the stretch in 2023, to the defensive side. With Davis back and Bozzi healthy, the

Big Red was amassing an impressive array of talent. Box was earning minutes, as was six-feet-three sophomore TJ Lamb, from West Chester, Pennsylvania, a onetime basketball standout at Episcopal Academy, and Gilmartin. Super senior Kyle Smith was available as well; he had logged serious minutes in the run to the championship game in 2022. The Big Red beat Albany, 18–11, with the seemingly requisite six goals from Kirst. After the game, most of the thoughts were with another captain and the comeback from Davis. "I didn't think I'd be able to play again," he says. "But our training staff, Ed Kelly and Danielle Hemly, did an amazing job. I honestly didn't know what my role would be." His role included more than on-field contributions. "It's one of the most remarkable things I've ever seen," Graham says. Added Stevens, "Chris never lost faith, even though any other human being would have. Chris Davis is a fucking warrior."

On Saturday, April 5, Cornell traveled to Providence, Rhode Island, to face Brown. Two days before the game, according to *Lacrosse Magazine*'s Justin Feil, first-year coach Jon Torpey held a one-quarter scrimmage, starters against the scout team. The winners earned the right to start against the number-one team in the nation. The scout team won. The regular starting lineup entered the game early in the first quarter, trailing 1–0, and did not do enough to stop Cornell's 13–9 victory. But the game was tied in the fourth quarter, and Torpey sent a message heard by much of lacrosse. "There's people out there that I'm sure are like, well, it probably cost you something in the game," Torpey told *Lacrosse Magazine*. "But I think if you look at the level of engagement from our lowest guy on the depth chart to the guys up the team and you come and see the compete level of practice and you see just how intense their focus is on stuff during the course of game week and how competitive things get and the cauldron that it creates at practice, you'd be like, man, it was probably worth it to do it."

By this point, word had begun to leak through the Ivy League that Kirst was dealing with an injury of some sort. In Providence, a visiting doctor evaluated Kirst before the game but left the examination door open, and a Brown player's mother happened to pass by at that moment. Word soon spread among the lacrosse mothers Kirst was dealing with an injury of some sort, with Michael Long's mother in New Jersey receiving a call a few days after the Brown game. Longtime Cornell observers, even if they did not know the extent, also would have known something was amiss. During pregame stretches the Cornell players leave their gloves and helmets and lacrosse sticks lying next to them. Given Kirst's PVC piping cast around his right hand, that was not an option. So the players kept their gloves on during the routine. Also, before every game, team captains meet with referees and the opposing captains at midfield and shake hands. For Kirst, taking off his glove to shake hands and reveal the cast, or not putting on the cast and risking an injury with a hard hand squeeze from an opponent, was not possible. It meant Kirst no longer joined the other captains and referees for the pregame meeting.

Cornell soon left to face fourth-ranked Syracuse on Saturday, April 12, at the neutral site location of Uniondale, New York. The night before the game, Walker Wallace was asked to deliver the senior speech. He had prepared for the night for years. Starting as a freshman, he would jot down ideas as they came to him of what he would say or scribble notes from senior speeches he found particularly impactful or funny. On April 11, Wallace used almost none of his rehearsed material. He began by recounting the story of him as a ten-year-old, writing down on a piece of paper, "I will play Division I lacrosse." He kept the note at his bedside and recited it aloud every night for eight years. At Cornell, he put the practice away. Until this year. He told teammates he recently wrote on a piece of paper the following phrase: "We will win a national title for Cornell lacrosse." He read it aloud every night. "That was a moment I wanted to share with them," Wallace says. "Obviously we were focused on Syracuse, but I wanted them to know, this is what I do every single night. This is what I think about every single night. Because I believe it in my whole heart. We are going to win a national title for Cornell. This is the team to do it." Wallace also shared his travels to watch Cornell games while older brother Fleet Wallace played. The younger Wallace would watch the warmup drills, watch the team interact. Here, too, he revealed something. "All I ever wanted," Wallace says, "was to be part of this team."

The next day, Cornell jumped to an 8–2 lead, thanks to three goals from Kirst. The Orange closed the deficit to three in the final minute when Kelleher scored for a 16–12 advantage. As Cornell tried to run out the clock, Kirst and his ailing right hand absorbed check after check from a frustrated defender. A second defender joined in. Buczek, sensing danger, called a time-out. Kirst and his teammates began seriously jawing with the Syracuse players, and both teams had to be separated. In the final seconds, a Syracuse defender hacked Goldstein on the arm. The referee threw a penalty flag, though play continued until the opposing team gained possession. The ball reached Wallace at midfield. The Syracuse goalie was out of the goal, trying to force a turnover. With eleven seconds left and the outcome decided, Wallace launched a fifty-yard shot. It went in, the final goal of a contentious 17–12 victory. Kirst again led the way with five goals. The secondary storyline to Cornell trying to end its forty-eight-year drought was Kirst's climb atop the NCAA all-time goal scoring charts. After the Syracuse game, he had 219 career goals, drawing closer to the record of 224 set by Virginia's Payton Cormier from 2020 to 2024.

To Kirst, the scoring record wasn't secondary; it wasn't even on his radar. "He's the best player in the world," Kelleher says, "and he doesn't have an ego." Added Howley, "When your best player is also your hardest worker, you're going to have a good team." To this point, Kirst still was not taking part in practice, one of the more remarkable notes about his ascent up the goal-scoring charts. Smith recalled one drill where Kirst participated and received a hard check on his right hand. Smith immediately apologized. No, Kirst told him. I'm going to see that in a game. I have to be ready.

On Saturday, April 19, Cornell traveled to Cambridge, Massachusetts, to play Harvard. Kirst entered with 54 goals on the season and 219 for his career. The Crimson closed to 12–11 on a goal early in the third quarter. Cornell answered with an 8–0 run, culminating in a goal by Kirst with six minutes to play for a 20–11 lead. It was his fifth goal of the game, tying Cormier's record. Watching on TV at home, LaFalce urged the final six minutes to go quickly. "I wanted CJ to break the record in Ithaca," he says. "That six minutes [in Cambridge] couldn't go fast enough." The game ended with no further scoring from the Big Red, 20–12 victors. Kirst entered the home finale, senior day, the following week, with 224 career goals. In their house on North Quarry Street during the week leading to the final regular season home game, there was plenty of talk about the goal-scoring record. It all came from Graham. Sitting on the sofa, he told anyone who would listen that the record would be his—he planned to go from his current total of eight goals to the NCAA record all in one afternoon.

Senior day arrived, Saturday, April 26, and the game against Dartmouth. In the Crescent parking lot, parents mixed their newest specialty concoction, a Schoellkopf Squeeze, with vodka, a splash of Chambord, three types of lemonade—sparkling, fresh squeezed, and sugar free—plus honeydew melon balls and fresh mint. Lohnes handed out her pins, which featured a giant Cornell Bear with a mallet dripping in green slime and the words "Smash the Big Green!" Another pin, smaller and less opponent-centric, fit the occasion. Red with white letters and black trim, looking like a remnant from the 1980s, it simply read, "Better than you found it." Kirst set the goal-scoring record after ten seconds, on an assist from Long, a much better collaboration than the one in the dining hall weeks earlier, after Kirst's worst fears on his hand injury were confirmed. The Big Red won, 10–8. Afterward came the senior day celebrations. Kirst walked to midfield with his mother, Michelle, and brothers Connor and Colin. Numerous other family members and friends were in the stands. "It was good to get [the record] out of the way," Kirst says. "Get it out of my head. That was a special moment for sure. To have it on senior day, senior night, was so much fun to celebrate." Cornell finished the regular season with a 12–1 record, and one team goal, finally, could be crossed off the list: Cornell was the Ivy League regular season champion and would host the four-team conference tournament starting on Friday, May 2.

Entering the Ivy semifinal against Yale, the Big Red was navigating injuries to its shortstick defenders. Bozzi and Box had injuries that were not severe, but they were held out of the two-games-in-three-days format as a precaution. Cornell had clinched a spot in the eighteen-team NCAA tournament field. All that was left to determine was its seeding. Among the noninjured, incredibly, was Davis. He proved such a good option Cornell no longer needed to slide to his matchup; essentially, Davis did not need the help of a double-team to keep his opponent in check. "The shortstick d-middies were a little bit in disarray until Chris Davis came back," says Andy Phillips. "He really shored up that unit. You cannot be an elite defense unless you're strong in that area." On the field during warm-ups before the Ivy semifinal, Gilmartin approached Davis. "They're going to have to pull us off this field," Gilmartin said, "before we come off." Also in the rotation were Lamb, Kyle Smith, and a pair of converted longstick midfielders, Reeder and junior Eddie Rayhill. "I handed Eddie Rayhill a shortstick at the most pivotal part of the season," Stevens says. "His response was, 'I'm going to be the best shortstick middie for two weeks, then go back [to longstick midfield].' Those guys were so dedicated to each other." Kyle Smith's playing time was severely curtailed by the return of Davis. It didn't matter. He was too pleased to see his classmate, teammate, and close friend back on the field. "It crossed my mind he'd never play again," Smith says. "We all sort of accepted it. Then in the snap of a finger he was good again. And he didn't miss a beat." Added Bozzi, "Seeing Chris back out on the field gave new life to a team that was already doing pretty well."

Cornell defeated Yale in the semifinals and Princeton in the title game, two important victories in forty-eight hours. Cornell gave up twenty-nine goals—fourteen to Yale, fifteen to Princeton—and forced Stevens into the unusual maneuver of switching to a zone defense to slow down the opposing offenses. Late in the victory over Yale, Cornell alum Jarett Wait captured a photo of a perfectly formed rainbow over Schoellkopf Field. After the semifinal win, the team was granted the rare treat of using the Cornell men's hockey training facilities to recover. Following the 20–15 victory over Princeton in the Ivy League final, a second team goal was crossed off the list. Cornell Athletic Director Nicki Moore held out the Ivy League trophy, waiting for the Cornell players to sweep it off her hands. None of the players obliged. Cascadden, standing nearby, finally explained it to her. "We felt bad, but I told her, 'Doctor Moore, that's not the trophy we want,'" Cascadden says. "'You may as well take it. We're not touching any trophy unless it's the national championship trophy.'"

8

THE HURRICANE

At 11:58 a.m. on Sunday, May 11, the day of Cornell's NCAA tournament first-round game against Albany, Mike French sent a text message. It went to five recipients, the captains of the Cornell team—CJ Kirst, Michael Bozzi, Chris Davis, Mikey Long, and Walker Wallace. "Guys, good luck today and throughout the tournament," French began. "As freshmen you've been there before, but this time is much different. You are by far the best team in the country, and a significant reason for that is your teamwork, leadership, and the selfless play you exhibit sets an example that makes everyone—past players, alumni, parents and friends—so proud. I see how you support and love each other. Thank you so much for that. This is a very special group coming from a very special place. The championship is your destiny. And I can't wait to witness the joy it will bring to everyone. LGR! MF."

A couple captains responded immediately; by midafternoon, all five had done so. The first-round game at Schoellkopf Field was a watershed in many ways, especially for sixth-year senior Michael Long. He had attended Cornell games as a child. His father, Steve, was one of the rare Cornell lacrosse alums who had scored a crucial goal against the team. After one year on the B team and two years as a reserve and battling injuries, as a senior in 1987, Steve Long proved an integral part of the squad that went undefeated until Memorial Day and the one-goal title game loss to Johns Hopkins. In 1988, Long joined a handful of other recent Cornell alums and played for the New York Athletic Club (NYAC). Richie Moran scheduled a scrimmage between the Big Red and NYAC in April, a way to test his current team without risking a blemish on its won-loss record. NYAC arrived in

Ithaca with twelve players, meaning for the entire sixty minutes it would have one substitute. Make that sixty-plus minutes, because the scrimmage went into overtime. In the extra session, Long, who had scored one goal in his college career, scored the winning goal. NYAC teammate Howard Borkan says for weeks afterward, Moran refused to talk to him and Long. "I'd call Richie," Borkan says, "and as soon as he heard my voice the line could go 'click,' because he'd hung up." The scrimmage loss compelled Moran to juggle his lineup and make some moves. The Big Red responded by reaching the 1988 title game before losing to Syracuse. The 1988 semifinal victory over Virginia was Moran's last NCAA playoff win.

Mikey Long says growing up in Mendham, New Jersey, around thirty miles from New York City, he never rooted for an NFL team, minus the Arizona Cardinals, where a relative worked; he never had a favorite college football team, nor a Major League Baseball team, nor an NHL or NBA team. His athletic favorites rested only with Cornell lacrosse. From a young age, he and his father would travel the East Coast following the Big Red with a fervor usually reserved for devotees of the Grateful Dead or Phish. In the early morning of March 7, 2015, Steve and Mikey, then in eighth grade, piled into their car in Mendham. They drove seven hours to Charlottesville for the top-ten showdown between Cornell and Virginia. With impending bad weather, the contest was moved to the University Hall artificial turf field, a gaudy blue surface with aluminum bleachers on one side and snow piled along the sideline. The forecast did not scare away the eighth-grader and his father; plus with the location change, the game would no longer be televised. Cornell's starting lineup that day included seniors Connor Buczek and Jordan Stevens. Cornell closed its deficit to 15–14 in the final minute but drew no closer. Buczek went one for twelve shooting, Stevens finished with one groundball and no caused turnovers. (In the stands a few rows behind Long and his father, though they didn't compare notes until years later, was Wallace; he and his family made the more reasonable one-hour trek from their home in Richmond.) With that, the Longs got in their car and drove back to Mendham, fourteen hours in one day to see a one-goal loss.

The Longs also branched out to attend the Crescent Lot pregame tailgate parties, in part because Steve Long and Joe Lizzio, the unofficial master of ceremonies for the cookouts, were college teammates. Mikey Long remembers trying to find someone to play catch with in the parking lot and nearly being rebuffed by a young Ryan Goldstein. "He was pretty stand-offish," Long says. "I still remind him of that sometimes." Superstitious as ever, the Longs found their way to the same seats in the same section at Schoellkopf Field. In the mid-2010s, it was the same row of bleachers as Gary Stevens, Jordan's father. They became quick friends. The elder Stevens was famous for bringing his wide-angle camera to games. He sometimes ventured into different parts of the stadium to snap pictures, often of the action on the field and Jordan playing defense, and always including photos of the father-and-son rooting for Cornell, which he uploaded to email and sent to Steve Long on Monday morning.

In the fall of the 2016–17 academic year, the picture for Mikey Long to play at Cornell became complicated. Long, then a sophomore at Delbarton School, broke his collarbone. He emerged from surgery weighing 107 pounds. One morning he was awakened by his father. "Get up," Steve Long said. "We're taking you to a physical trainer." By the start of his sophomore season in 2017, Long was lifting weights and eating as much as he could, and his weight was up to 160. He received playing time on a typically strong Delbarton squad. (Kirst, then a freshman at Delbarton, spent the year on junior varsity.) On September 1 of his junior year of high school, a handful of Division I programs contacted Long. Cornell was not one of them. "Mikey was beating down our door, but he was basically four-feet-nothing tall," says Jordan Stevens, then a Cornell assistant. "My dad remembered sitting with Mikey and his dad. He said they were good guys. Mikey was this cute little kid dragging his lacrosse stick around. He was an incredible student and a good player, but he was literally too small for us to consider. Over time, he kept working his butt off. And he clearly loves Cornell lacrosse more than anything. At some point [the coaches] just said, 'We're being idiots.'"

Other college programs were not ignoring the starting attackman, now 5-feet-10, 180 pounds. Long narrowed his choices to Villanova and Lehigh, both strong academic schools with good lacrosse. His mother, greatly impressed in her meetings with Buczek and Stevens, held out hope. Just hours before Mikey was set to make his choice, he heard from then-Cornell Coach Peter Milliman. On the line as well was Stevens. Milliman said he'd like to bring Long to campus. Long believed it was another invitation to see Cornell, which was the last thing he needed. Stevens, correctly gauging the lukewarm response, interjected. "Mikey, I don't think you understand," Stevens said. "Coach is offering you a spot on the team." Long immediately accepted, then raced to tell his parents.

Long became the Forrest Gump of recent Cornell lacrosse lore. He was present for and had a strong connection with almost every major moment. He was in the starting lineup in early March 2020 in Charlotte for the one-goal victory over Penn State and took part in the postgame celebration in the tiny high school stadium locker room. Though he was close friends with Kirst, his high school teammate, he was careful not to be too involved in Kirst's recruitment. "CJ's not great at making big decisions like that," Long says. "He slow-walked the whole thing. But at some point I was like, 'He's gotta follow me here.'" Long was on campus when the 2020 season was canceled and for the death of beloved trainer Jim Case, who had also worked with Steve Long. Mikey was on campus for the star-crossed 2021 nonseason. He was in the lineup for 2022, was on campus for

Moran's death, and started in the 2022 NCAA title game. In 2023 he battled a hamstring injury in the preseason and missed six games. The Big Red got off to a slow start. When Long returned, Cornell won five of its next six games before losing in overtime in the NCAA tournament first round. Toward the end of 2024, Cornell was playing well with Long in the lineup. Before the regular season finale, he tore his hamstring again. He was out for the rest of the year, even if Cornell made it to Philadelphia and Championship Weekend. As it was, Cornell didn't even make it out of Ithaca in losing to Penn in the Ivy semifinals. Long watched from the Cornell sideline, mere yards from where close friend Kirst was shoved in the back away from the action, then hit in the head, resulting in a two-minute penalty and causing his white number 15 jersey to be covered in blood. And that's where, in normal circumstances, Long's Cornell career would have ended. Two nights later, after the selection show, he would have sat around the C at midfield at Schoellkopf Field, reminiscing about his favorite days on campus and looking toward the next chapter.

In the fall of the 2023–24 academic year, Long realized he would be eligible for the following season as well. He was not, however, able to play as a graduate student at Cornell—the waiver from the 2021 cancellation had expired. Long was readying to graduate, enter the transfer portal and spend his sixth and final year of eligibility at one of the schools that had recruited him out of Delbarton.

Then Buczek reminded Long of what transpired at another Ivy League school a couple years earlier. A star lacrosse player intentionally left himself a few credits short of graduating, thus enabling him to spend his final year of eligibility in the Ivy League as he was not yet a grad student, despite having played for five years. "It was sort of a loophole," Long says, "and we decided to use it." It was still a strange existence, even by Long's admission. He would spend another fall semester away from Ithaca—in the fall of 2024 he worked at an internship with one of Kirst's uncles and, for extra money to put toward tuition, also worked as a caddy at a local golf club. But it meant he would be back in 2025, a member of the only sports team he had ever really followed, for one last run. "Mikey Long is the interesting one," says Tom LaFalce. "The narrative of this period of time is how much he was the glue of that offense. I think 2024 looks a lot different if he doesn't get hurt. They missed him. This year I kept thinking, as long as Mikey is healthy they have a real shot. I saw on TV against Harvard where he took a really hard hit to his shoulder and I thought, uh-oh, if there's one guy we can't really lose, it's him."

Long says now Cornell almost lost his services in 2025, though not against Harvard. A few weeks earlier, in the midseason victory over Yale, he took an awkward tumble to the turf and fell on the collarbone he had broken in high school. Long left the field with the help of a trainer and said he feared his season was over. X-rays at Yale's state-of-the-art stadium showed it was not broken but had received a jolt. For the rest of the year Long played through pain, sometimes unable to lift his arms above shoulder level. He insisted on remaining in the lineup. As he fielded calls from friends from high school and college who had moved on to their full-time jobs and were working in big cities across the country and experiencing different adventures, he patiently explained he had one more lacrosse season left. "I'm not sure they really understood," he says.

Albany entered the NCAA contest at Schoellkopf Field with a seven-game winning streak. Junior attackman Silas Richmond was the focal point. He had seven assists in an early season victory over Patriot League champion Colgate, and in the regular season meeting against Cornell added six points. Against the University of Massachusetts, Richmond scored on a one-handed shot with his back turned to the goalie. At six-feet-four, the British Columbia native would pose a big problem for Stevens and the defense, at a time when the Big Red gave up twenty-nine goals in two Ivy League tournament contests. The Great Danes also boasted sophomore Ryan Doherty, a strong left-handed shooter from New Hampshire. In a midseason victory over Hobart he scored nine goals, near a single-game NCAA record.

In the Crescent parking lot on Sunday, May 11, the concoction for Mother's Day was a Happy Mom, with grapefruit juice, two kinds of grapefruit-flavored sparkling water, honey, and, for the adventurous or very nervous, a dash of vodka. Lohnes's spirit pins were "Beat Albany" and "Find a Way." With its zone defense at the ready, Stevens began with the trademark man-to-man. Senior Jayson Singer guarded Richmond, with junior Matt Dooley, the off-ball specialist, on Doherty, and junior Brendan Staub covering Johns Hopkins transfer Koleton Marquis. In the opening minutes, Richmond maneuvered around Singer and fired an underhand shot, a shot that looked like he was shoveling snow out of a driveway, past Knust for an early lead. Long and Kirst took over, scoring the next six Cornell goals. The Big Red won, 15–6. Kirst finished with six goals, giving him seventy-four for the season, close to the NCAA single-season record of eighty-two.

The University of Richmond was up next, in an NCAA quarterfinal on Saturday, May 17, at Hofstra University in Hempstead, New York. Cornell won the regular season meeting, 12–11, after falling behind early. The teams were practically a mirror image of each other. Borkan, a longtime lacrosse observer and former college coach, noted Cornell ran an offense influenced by Mike Messere, the longtime coach at West Genesee High outside Syracuse. Jeff Tambroni played for Messere in high school and brought the offense with him to Cornell. Despite a few tweaks here and there—Milliman added a Canadian box-lacrosse influence, for instance—it was largely still the West Genny/Messere offense.

Richmond Coach Dan Chemotti also graduated from West Genesee, and not only did he implement Messere's offense but the two would also meet every year at Thanksgiving and Christmas, Chemotti spending hours with his mentor, going over film and taking notes. At times it's an up-tempo, pass-and-move scheme, trying to draw attention to the ball carrier with an off-ball cutter often left open for a point-blank shot. If the immediate offensive opportunity isn't available, the next plan is to hold the ball as long as possible, setting constant picks to find a mismatch while working the clock. The ploy was similar to the Big Red's approach. "I lost count," says LaFalce, "of how many times Mikey Long got matched against a shortstick. Every time I looked up he was guarded by another one."

Borkan listed further similarities. Both teams had a slick off-ball finisher from Canada. For Cornell and Willem Firth (thirty goals on seventy-two shots, 41.6 percent), Richmond boasted junior Lucas Littlejohn and his forty goals and 46.5 percent shooting. Both also had a powerful presence as a dodging midfielder, senior Joe Sheridan for Richmond (twenty-eight goals) and senior Hugh Kelleher for Cornell (twenty-four goals). On defense, Richmond coordinator Paul Richards previously had been at Cornell. He brought with him the scheme that worked so well in Ithaca. Both programs rely heavily on their shortstick defenders to be aggressive, to pick up the offensive midfielder high in the zone. The risks are one, the defenders will become tired, and two, it gives more space for a skilled midfielder to beat his defender. Cornell and Richmond were willing to take that risk in exchange for unsettling the offense, and there would be enough depth in the defensive midfield to keep players fresh. Cornell and Richmond also protected the paint, to use a basketball term; they focused on keeping the offense outside of the ten yards or so directly in front of the goal, leaving open lower-angle, lower-percentage shots. The Spiders boasted victories over national powers Georgetown, Virginia, and North Carolina. The defense featured junior Hunter Smith from Rochester, New York, one of the best on-ball defenders in the nation, the Atlantic 10 Conference defenseman of the year; senior Mitchell Dunham from Hamilton, Ontario, a wizard at getting his stick into passing lanes, who had five caused turnovers in the win over the Hoyas; and senior Jack Pilling from Upper Derby, Pennsylvania, one of the top shortstick defenders in the nation.

Two other subplots entered the picture. One came into focus the day before the game. During the Friday walkthrough practice at Hofstra, Knust struggled to see the ball during warm-ups as it was coming out of the stick of Max Tennant, Cornell's assistant coach, a onetime standout at Division III Ohio Wesleyan. Knust says he struggled tracking the ball against the gray background imposed by the metal bleachers in the north end zone and in the south end zone, where the background was a beige brick administrative building with large tinted windows.

The other subplot came when *Inside Lacrosse* published its anonymous scouting reports, detailing quotes from Division I coaches on all eight quarterfinal teams. The report for Cornell made for particularly pointed reading. Under Kirst's name came this: "Is he playing hurt? That would explain why he isn't dodging as much as he was earlier in the season." Kirst's broken hand had flown under the radar for much of lacrosse, not least because he was still scoring at an incredible clip. Also because of the lengths Cornell went to make sure it was not obvious he was playing with a cast. Now, the specter of his injury was out in the open.

The night before the game, Cornell's players, coaches, and staff ate dinner in the main dining room at Vincent's Clam Bar in Carle Place, New York. The menu included chicken parmesan, pasta, chicken Francese, rice balls, and several dessert options. Also on tap was a little good-natured, if slightly awkward, heckling from celebrity chef and actor Joseph Gannascoli, best known for his role in HBO's *The Sopranos*. Gannascoli was at the restaurant signing copies of his new book. On his way out, Buczek signed several Cornell lacrosse T-shirts for employees, then pointed the team to the Long Island Marriott in Uniondale. Before going to bed, before reading aloud his note about winning a national title for Cornell, Wallace, the Richmond native, had one other thought. "I was hoping we wouldn't have to play Richmond," he says. "They're very similar to us. Very good fundamentals, really tough in the middle of the field, they make non-highlight plays. We knew it was going to be a 'big boy game.'"

May 17 arrived warm and muggy in Hempstead. The crowd of 8,209 included hundreds of Cornell fans. A couple hours before the game, they gathered in the north parking lot next to Earle Ovington Boulevard. The pregame drink was a Creased Mike French, essentially an Arnold Palmer with a twist: three parts Chick-Fil-A lemonade, two parts Chick-Fil-A unsweetened tea, simple syrup, crushed ice, and, for those battling nerves before the huge game, a dash of sweet tea vodka. Lohnes's pin encouraged Cornell to "Squash the Spiders" along with another that said "Rinse/Repeat." Many fans at Hofstra wore red "Big Red 15" T-shirts, an homage to Kirst's uniform number, Cornell's nickname, and Kirst's red hair. The shirts were the brainchild of Wait and sold as a fundraiser for the CityLax charity. Inside the stadium, Cornell took the field for warm-ups in their gray Teagle T-shirts with red shorts and red helmets.

Richmond warmed up in its white T-shirts with the word "GAS" on the bottom, a reference to the team's motto: all gas, no brakes. The game began with Smith covering Kirst on one end; at the other, junior Matt Dooley covered Littlejohn. Cornell scored the first goal, Goldstein from Long. Richmond answered. Midway through the first quarter, Cornell showed its enviable depth at short-stick defender when sophomore TJ Lamb fired a rocket shot in transition past

Richmond's goalie for a 2-1 lead. Cornell rotated its shortstick defenders, Davis and Box in one pairing, Bozzi and Lamb in another, to keep them fresh. The fresh legs did not immediately pay dividends. Early in the second quarter Richmond led 6-4; to that point, Knust had made only three saves. With less than four minutes left in the first half, Kirst took matters into his own hands and scored on a diving shot to close the deficit to 6-5, which was the score at halftime.

Knust's fears of the previous day were coming true—by his own admission, he was not seeing the ball. In the first half he made only four saves. The good news for Cornell's defense was the depth at the shortstick position, and Dooley had kept the high-scoring Littlejohn without a shot, let alone a goal. On the first two possessions of the second half Richmond scored twice and led 8-5. Littlejohn also finally took his first shot—it went wide—before Dooley went back to limiting the sharpshooter's looks. Kirst, by this point, was not shooting well, one for six. In the press box, Borkan remembers thinking Kirst's injury was his ankle and not his hand. "He kept shooting a little high," Borkan says. "That's usually an ankle [injury]." Richmond's goalie, grad student Zach Vigue, was tremendous throughout. In one stretch in the third quarter, with Richmond leading 9-8, Kirst and Long took good shots; Vigue saved both, but the Big Red retained possession to reset the shot clock to sixty seconds. On the same possession, Goldstein hit the goal pipe; again the Big Red got the loose ball, again the sixty-second shot clock reset. The Big Red switched midfield personnel. Out went the second line; in came the starters. Dalton took a good shot. Vigue made another save. Another loose ball, another Cornell groundball, another reset. The stalemate ended after three minutes and thirty seconds, and with Richmond senior Michael Farrell grabbing a groundball and clearing it. Richmond's sideline and its fans erupted. After the long possession and the immediate emotional spike on the Richmond sideline, it began to dawn on Cornell's fans, and at least some of the coaches and players, that the long possession drained much of the Spiders' gas tank. Playing so much defense in the warm sun, the unit looked exhausted.

Still, Richmond led at the end of the quarter, 10-9, adding to its collection of leads at the end of the first quarter and halftime. Cornell's players remember looking at the Richmond huddle in the break between the third and fourth quarters and seeing players doubled over or kneeling on their haunches, drinking water and seeking cold towels. Cornell countered with an old axiom from Coach Tom Howley: no fear, no fatigue, no frustration. Never let the other team see any of those things. "We stood as tall as possible," said Graham. "Shoulders back, heads high."

In the vital fourth quarter, as the second-most precious commodity, the time remaining in the game, became important, Cornell scored goals on four of its first eight possessions. The goals came from Dalton, Firth, and Kirst and culminated in a score by Dalton again for a 13–12 lead with five minutes twenty-eight seconds remaining. The scoring streak coincided with numerous changes among Richmond's defensive personnel. Smith, the Nike Lacrosse Second-Team Media All-American guarding Kirst, went in and out of the game, seemingly battling both fatigue and a cramp (when on the sideline he received near-constant treatment on his thigh and upper leg). Dunham was on the sideline on the possession that led to Dalton's third goal and the 13–12 lead. Richmond's standout shortstick defenders, who had gone step for step with Cornell, began to give up crucial ground in the fourth quarter. When asked after the game if there had been a sense the Richmond players had started to tire, Kirst nodded his head as Buczek answered. "I don't know if there was a sense," he said. "We just trust what's in our tank. We have the best strength coach in the game and the guy that really gives us a lot of belief that we are ready to compete in big moments." On Dalton's goal to make it 13–12, Pilling, the star shortstick defender, was a step slow to reach Long, and it gave Long the crucial extra second to fire his laser pass to a wide-open Dalton.

Still, Cornell was not out of danger just yet. Knust had not made a save in the final fourteen-plus minutes of the third quarter and none so far in the fourth, 28 minutes without a save. On Richmond's first possession trailing 13–12, one shot went wide and another was blocked, and the shot clock expired. Richmond's second possession trailing by a goal never got started after Kirst forced a failed clear to give the Big Red the ball back. The Spiders still trailed by a goal in the final minute when they forced a shot clock violation. They cleared the ball and called a time-out with twenty-seven seconds left. On the Richmond sideline, Chemotti and his staff did quick calculations. The most recent three goals had come from midfielders—Sheridan with two and senior Lukas Olsson with one. Those two took the field, joined by sophomore Gavin Creo, and the starting attack. Sheridan was to look to Olsson on the right wing, for Olsson to either shoot or pass to Littlejohn, held to one shot by Dooley. A shot of any kind would have been opportune; Knust had not made a save in more than twenty-nine minutes.

On the Cornell sideline, the coaches opted for a change. For the first time, the Big Red, harkening back to the Ivy League tournament, went into a zone. "We wanted to throw a changeup," Buczek said. "We thought they might be expecting [man to man] and it might take a little time for them to adjust." Play resumed. Sheridan's pass on the far right wing tipped off Olsson's stick and led to a scrum similar to the halftime exhibition featuring two youth teams from nearby Massapequa. The clock ticked under fifteen seconds, then under ten. Neither Richmond nor Cornell gained control. As the clock hit under two seconds, Cornell's players began storming the field. The ball remained on the ground. The game was over. "Coming out of that timeout, we were looking to run a play that we've run a million times," Chemotti said. "We tried to disguise it a little bit. . . . We had an open guy and Joe made the right look.... If those guys had been able to connect I think Lukas Olsson had a good shot there. It was the right play."

The Big Red won an NCAA quarterfinal in which Knust made one second-half save. Kirst went two for thirteen shooting and made his presence felt elsewhere, with game highs in caused turnovers (three) and groundballs (ten), even more than face-off specialist Jack Cascadden, who tilted the field in Cornell's favor by winning seventeen of twenty-five face-offs and adding nine groundballs. Essentially, Kirst had impacted the game making the so-called Boiardi plays, earning a few "21's" for the white board in the Schoellkopf Field film room. It also proved once again Kirst's penchant to impact a game in ways far beyond scoring. "All the money players showed up," Wait said. "CJ's groundballs and caused turnover at the end of the game were unbelievable." The crucial plays on offense came from Dalton. It was his first career game with three goals. The player cut from his grade school team, and playing junior varsity in grades nine and ten in Canada, scored the goal that sent Cornell to the NCAA semifinals in Foxborough. "Dalts came up huge," Graham said. In the second game, Princeton and Syracuse was more of a track meet than a lacrosse game, a 19-18 Orange victory in a game that featured 93 shots and never went more than four minutes without a goal.

The following day in Annapolis, and in the second round of NCAA quarterfinals at Navy-Marine Corps Memorial Stadium, organizers were hopeful for a big crowd for a doubleheader featuring Penn State against two-time defending champion Notre Dame and Georgetown against Maryland. Early in the week, Navy officials said the number of presold tickets reached 5,000. By Thursday, the number was 5,500. Fingers crossed for an attendance of 8,000 people. By Friday, the presale eclipsed 8,000, then 9,000. On Saturday, the promising weather forecast held, and the first set of quarterfinals at Hofstra turned into all-time great games. Suddenly the presale at Navy reached 10,000, then 10,500, then 11,000. By the end, the presale was around 13,000; the games drew 17,721. Penn State came back from a six-goal third-quarter deficit to win, 14–12. Its zone defense held Notre Dame without a shot on goal for the final nineteen-plus minutes, an unheard-of stat at the sport's highest level. Maryland won the second quarterfinal with a perfunctory 9–6 victory over Georgetown. The field for Foxborough was set: Penn State against Cornell in the first semifinal, followed by Maryland against Syracuse.

On Monday, May 19, back in Ithaca Cornell's players began their preparations for the semifinal. Knust walked into a meeting with Stevens, hailing him with a quick "Hey coach, I'm good, I'm doing fine." The shaky performance on Saturday was gone. "I remember telling him, 'Damn right you're good,'" Stevens says. "'If you thought I was questioning you for one damn second, you're crazy.'" The rest of the week went as planned. Cornell's preseason goals included a victory over Penn State; that had gone by the boards in early March in a shocking overtime loss. Now the Big Red had another chance. Kirst was still dealing with his broken hand—surgery now appeared set for early June, after the season and before he moved into the Premier Lacrosse League. The Philadelphia Waterdogs made him the number-one pick, knowing full well he'd miss several weeks while recovering from surgery. Long, too, was dealing with his collarbone and shoulder issues, yet he fully intended on playing in the semifinal.

On Friday morning, the team traveled by bus to Foxborough, Massachusetts. They checked into the Hilton Garden Inn Patriot Place Hotel and practiced inside Gillette Stadium, home of the NFL's New England Patriots. The organization offered more than a state-of-the-art facility. Sophomore Matty Tully, Cornell's backup goalie and a Foxborough native, arrived at his locker and was startled to find a New England Patriots blue number 55 jersey, Tully's number on Cornell. (Tufts junior Declan Murphy, another Foxborough native and set to play in the Division III title game on Sunday, also received a Patriots jersey.) As the team left the locker room for its walkthrough practice, Smith, a lifelong Patriots fan, took the field raising his arms up and down in the manner of star quarterback Tom Brady; nearby, the Cornell lacrosse contingent yelled and cheered. "It sounds like it was kind of cheesy," Smith says, "but it felt awesome." Knust remembers taking warm-up shots from Tennant and immediately seeing the ball well against the backdrop of navy blue seats in both end zones.

After practice and quick showers at the hotel, the team headed to its dinner at an expensive Italian restaurant not far from the stadium. Most of the so-called super seniors found themselves at the same table—Caddigan, Wallace, Davis, Long, Kirst, and Sheehan. The players and staff, burned out on chicken parmesan and pasta and salad, were thrilled to see the restaurant's offerings of either veal chop or steak. "We all decided to go with the veal chop because it looked bigger than the steak," Caddigan says. "It ended up being terrible. We were so bummed. I think Walker Wallace when he got back to his hotel room ordered a steak for delivery." Overall, though, not even a subpar veal chop could ruin the moment. "I'll never forget those pregame dinners," Caddigan says. "Some of those times, I've never laughed so hard in my life."

On Friday afternoon, May 23, as the Cornell players went through their walkthrough practice, Lizzio arrived at his favorite butcher, Pino's Prime Meat, on Sullivan Street in the Soho section of Manhattan. The Big Red had not won a title in 48 years, and Lizzio wanted to make sure the pregame and postgame spreads were fitting for what might take place. He arrived to pick up his order for the next day's tailgate party, in parking lot 3B of Gillette Stadium. The order was as follows: 10 Wagyu tomahawk steaks; 100 hot sausages; 100 Merguez sausages; 152 marinated lamb chops; 30 chicken thighs; 32 skirt steaks; and several huge ribeye steaks. Lizzio loaded the food into coolers and made his way up Interstate 95. By this point, he had already called Pulcinella, his favorite Italian deli in his native Massapequa, and ordered the following, also for the semifinal tailgate: thirty-six Italian footlong heroes, or subs; thirty-six American cold-cut subs; seven orders of veal meatballs; four orders of rice balls; five orders of penne pasta with vodka sauce; two orders of *orecchiette baresi*, an Italian pasta, sausage, and vegetables dish; four orders of chicken parmesan; four orders of stuffed shells; five orders of shrimp oreganata, an Italian-American dish; three platters of Greek salads; two orders of rigatoni and Bolognese sauce; two Caesar salad platters; two orders of roasted potatoes; three hundred orders of fresh bread; and several orders of fresh vegetables. This was to be delivered by the deli. To do so, manager Beth, accompanied by four workers—including her sons and grandsons, who served as caterers—would hit the road for Foxborough at three o'clock Saturday morning. Lizzio warned Beth he would repeat the order for Monday, assuming Cornell won its semifinal, but for superstitious reasons, he did not dare place the order just yet.

Around the time Lizzio and his carful of coolers left Sullivan Street, Lohnes and her husband, Tim, and their two younger sons boarded their flight to Boston. Lohnes, not normally a nervous traveler, acknowledged being jittery on May 23. She had packed her pin maker in her suitcase and was worried TSA would think it was a weapon. She packed the button machine because she made pins only for the semifinal; doing buttons for the title game, with Cornell yet to advance, would have invited massively bad luck. If Cornell won, she brought with her the makings for four hundred pins for Monday. Saturday's offerings were "We Are Big Red," a play on the famed chant of their semifinal opponents, "We are Penn State!" For the more motivational pin, Lohnes says after 17 games she was running out of ideas. She recalled a recent interview with Long in which he said the offense needed to "level up," a term from video games meaning to improve enough to advance to the next level. For this, she made a white background with a red "Level Up." She also created a pin with "Cornell Lacrosse: A Way of Life," complete with the program's hard hat and Boiardi's number 21 on the side. "There's something nostalgic about associating pins with major events," Lohnes says. "Think about campaign pins for [political] elections. People are looking to have a little joy in their life, and sometimes a silly, small thing can make a difference." The button machine made its way through security. With that, she and her family boarded their flight.

Around the time the flight attendants were doing their final check before takeoff, a story broke on social media: Sources said the NCAA was set to announce the host of the following year's Championship Weekend. It originally was slated to be back in Foxborough. That changed after the United States won the bidding to cohost the 2026 FIFA World Cup. Gillette Stadium made the list of venues, as did Lincoln Financial Field in Philadelphia, another frequent lacrosse location. The announcement of the new 2026 Championship Weekend host especially sent shockwaves through the Cornell faithful, because the NCAA selected Charlottesville, Virginia, and the University of Virginia's Scott Stadium. The coincidence was unmistakable. The last time Cornell won the title, in 1977, it did so at Scott Stadium.

Saturday, May 24, arrived overcast and cool. Many in the early morning crowd in parking lot 3B wore jackets. The Cornell team boarded the bus to the stadium a little before 10 a.m. for the noon game. The Hilton Garden Inn Patriot Place is within walking distance, so close players said they could hear the crowd noise from their rooms. Still, taking the bus, even for a one-minute drive, was selected for a reason. As the bus pulled out of the hotel parking lot, the driver decided to take a slightly longer route. His chosen path took the players, coaches, and staff past lot 3B. There, two hours before the opening face-off, they saw hundreds and hundreds of Cornell alumni, family, and friends, almost all wearing red. Someone alerted the throng that the team bus was approaching. The noise the fans made was so loud it shook the vehicle's windows. Players lost in their own thoughts, listening to music through their headphones, suddenly turned the music off, removed their headphones, and took in the whole scene. They picked out their family members, their friends, mentors from previous teams, and the guys who had hosted them on recruiting trips, encouraged them to finish one of Howley's strenuous workouts, or called them out for not going all the way to the endline on a sprint. Ending the national title drought, beating Penn State, giving their all for Cornell today—it was all in front of them, and they had the support of thousands behind them. The bus swept like Aladdin's carpet past the fans and into the stadium. The tailgate party resumed.

Kevin Moran, son of longtime coach Richie Moran, said there were so many friends, former teammates and players from his father's era he hadn't seen in years that in roughly ninety minutes he never actually made it to Lizzio's food. LaFalce, not calling games on TV or the radio, and instead attending as a fan, packed in his suitcase a Penn State sweatshirt in deference to his older son, a sophomore at the school playing intramural lacrosse. On this morning the elder LaFalce was wearing Cornell gear on his body—and his heart on his sleeve. "I remember my wife saying, 'If they don't win it this year,'" he says, "'I don't know what I'm going to do.'" LaFalce made the rounds at the pregame tailgate party, shocked at the turnout, the sheer number of Cornell fans assembled at 10 a.m. in an asphalt parking lot in a Boston suburb on a holiday weekend. He says one other thing struck him that morning: how many of the young boys running around with their red-clad parents were named George.

Inside the stadium, Cornell and Penn State went through their warm-ups. Cornell took the field in white jerseys, red shorts, and red helmets. Penn State wore blue jerseys with white helmets and white shorts. The Nittany Lions entered with a 12-4 record and senior Matt Traynor, the star attackman who missed the game in Ithaca, was back in the lineup. Not only was he back, he scored six goals in the quarterfinal win over Notre Dame and had scored nine goals in the NCAA tournament, the most of any player. He would be guarded by Singer. Buczek took the field wearing a red baseball cap with Boiardi's 21 on it; another assistant wore a red baseball cap with McEneaney's 10. Finally, the clock struck noon. ESPN's cameras surveyed the scene. After the national anthem, the game began. In the opening face-off, Penn State freshman Reid Gillis won the draw and pushed the ball past Cascadden and into the open field. The Nittany Lions had a fast break. In the opening seconds, Gillis took a point-blank shot, overhand and low. Knust made the save. The shaky performance of the previous week, no saves in the final 29 minutes, was gone. "It was a great way to settle in," Knust says. Defense dominated the opening passages. In one possession, Penn State's leading goal scorers, Traynor and redshirt freshman Liam Matthews, fired lefty shots at Knust. He saved both. Later, freshman phenom Hunter Aquino came off a screen and had a wide-open look from 12 yards. He fired a textbook overhand shot, and Knust saved that as well. At the other end, Cornell struggled for any good shots. It took nearly twelve minutes for the Big Red's first on-goal attempt, and that shot, from Long, was saved by redshirt senior Jack Fracyon. In the final seconds of the first quarter, Firth made an off-ball cut, the defense was not aware, and he scored the opening goal on a point-blank finish, assisted by Long. Penn State scored twice to open the second quarter. Cascadden, winless in four face-off attempts, won the draw and scored to tie the game at 2. Back and forth it went. The Nittany Lions jumped to a 4–2 lead. Goals from Long and Kelleher tied it, though Kirst had yet to get going offensively. Penn State led 5–4 at halftime, with Kirst having not scored a goal yet. Early in the third quarter, defenseman Brendan Staub scored in transition for Cornell to tie the game. Then Kelleher scored on a rocket shot from about fifteen yards, a jump shot high to high.

By this point, it was clear Kelleher was in semifinal mode, looking as he had in 2022, in the blowout victory over Rutgers, when he scored three goals and broke the lacrosse sticks of two defenders. To counter Kelleher, and because Cascadden won six consecutive face-offs, early in the third quarter Penn State went to its zone defense. The previous weekend, it had helped erase the six-goal deficit against Notre Dame, had held the Fighting Irish without a shot on goal in the crucial fourth quarter. The Nittany Lions broke out the zone against Cornell's second midfield—Sheehan, junior Brian Luzzi, and sophomore Ryan Waldman. Waldman fired a shot stick-side on Fracyon that went in. Cornell led, 7–6. To this point, Kirst was zero for four shooting, with two turnovers. And Cornell, somehow, had a one-goal lead. It became two goals after Staub fired a perfect pass in transition to a cutting Goldstein, who scored on a close shot for an 8–6 lead. Penn State scrapped its zone. Yet the lead grew to 9–6 after a goal by Luzzi, then 10–6 on a score by Long, after which Penn State, sensing the game was slipping away, called a time-out. Not yet in the scoring column was Kirst, who entered with 76 goals and a still-broken right hand.

In the fourth quarter, Penn State scored three consecutive goals—including a behind-the-back bounce shot from Matthews and a crank shot from Traynor on a fast break, a shot ESPN clocked at seventy-nine miles per hour—to draw within 10–9. The Nittany Lions had a remarkable comeback in the regular season win against Cornell and another in the quarterfinal victory against Notre Dame. At the other end of the field, twirling his stick in annoyance with himself, Kirst was still without a goal or assist. Kirst was missing shots by inches. In soccer, the old saying goes, sometimes the ball turns its back on you. It had happened to Kirst in the Ivy League semifinal in 2024, the ugly, bloody, season-ending loss to Penn, and it happened again in Foxborough. Nothing was working. The teams traded possessions when Cornell had the ball with around six minutes to play and a one-goal lead. Penn State was back in its zone defense. Kelleher caught a pass, with room to take two steps and fire a hard overhand textbook shot past Fracyon, clocked by ESPN at 88 miles per hour. Cornell led 11–9, with 5:49 remaining. It was Kelleher's third goal. Penn State's final four possessions featured a shot clock violation and two turnovers, one caused by Gilmartin, the other by Davis, the swarming shortstick defenders proving their mettle when it mattered most. (The fourth Penn State possession ended in a save by Knust.) In front of 31,524 fans, many wearing red and cheering every Cornell goal, the Big Red won, 11–9. As the game ended, Sheehan ran up to Kelleher and said it was the most dominating midfield performance he'd seen since Sergio Perkovic, a Notre Dame midfielder, scored five goals in the fourth quarter of the 2014 NCAA title game. It was needed even more given Kirst's struggles on offense. "We all knew at some point Huey was going to have a performance like that," Sheehan says. "Just a physically dominating performance. He's been a freak athlete the whole time he's been here, starting in his freshman year. . . . I remember watching him [against Penn State] and thinking wow, that's what a professional midfielder looks like." The other main cog in the offensive machine, Kirst, finished zero for seven shooting, with no assists and two turnovers. It was hard to tell in the locker room afterward.

"You'd have thought," Caddigan says, "he had scored twenty goals with twenty assists. He had a smile on his face the whole time." Cascadden was huge as well, winning fifteen of twenty-three face-offs and adding nine groundballs and a goal. Cornell was one victory from its first NCAA title since 1977.

After the game, Cornell's players showered and took the bus to parking lot 3B. They mingled with family and friends. Kirst was all smiles, posing for pictures with fans and their kids, signing autographs. "I had my seventh-grade son there," says Mike Levine. "They were running around the parking lot and then they said, 'There's CJ!' And they ran over to him. CJ was so gracious, with a big smile, taking pictures and signing T-shirts. I knew he didn't have a big game, I didn't realize he finished with zero points. And you certainly couldn't tell by how he was acting." The team soon headed back to the Hilton Garden Inn Patriot Place. They wanted to prepare for Monday's title game. The mingling could wait. As the team departed, Lizzio nudged Beth, the manager from Pulcinella, and asked for a repeat order for delivery on Monday morning. Lohnes prepared her spirit pin designs for the title game. Andy Phillips, driving back to Manhasset to take care of a not-yet-housetrained puppy, a white-haired pointing griffon named Griz, readied to watch the replay of the victory over Penn State. "I remember watching the game [in person] and thinking we looked frazzled and we were losing our poise," he said. "When I watched the replay, I realized the only one losing his poise was me. The team was purposeful, not perfect, but clearly in control. They were poised and purposeful, the identity of this team."

In the second semifinal, Maryland hammered Syracuse, 14–8. Logan McNaney finished with fourteen saves, and senior Eric Spanos, a six-feet-four attackman from Philadelphia, scored four goals. Memorial Day would feature the teams seeded numbers one and two and a rematch of the 1971, 1976, and 2022 title games. Borkan began predicting what Maryland would do on Monday, with one thought popping up again and again. "To me," Borkan says, "CJ not scoring should have been an alarm for Maryland. Because they were probably saying, 'Wow, this team can win without CJ Kirst scoring a goal.'"

Buck Briggs, Cornell class of 1976, could not attend Saturday. The semifinal coincided with Cornell's graduation, and Briggs hosts an annual graduation party at his house-cum-museum in Ithaca, the Old Stone Heap, built in 1820, a former tavern along the Ithaca Geneva Turnpike. The house lies a few miles from campus; from his backyard, Schoellkopf Field is clearly visible in the distance. Briggs's home includes dozens of Cornell athletics curios: jerseys and photos, helmets and lacrosse sticks and football cleats and even a giant scoreboard once used by Cornell. There also is a re-creation of the beloved Royal Palms Tavern, a Collegetown dive bar that sat at 209 Dryden Street for seventy-one years, before closing in 2012. Briggs's planned excursion for Monday was in jeopardy: His friend said he was driving to the game, with Briggs in tow, only if Cornell won and Syracuse lost. The friend explained he could not sit through another Syracuse-Cornell NCAA final in Foxborough—too many bad memories from 2009. After the second semifinal, Syracuse lost, and Briggs won a ride. By then, he had picked his wardrobe for Monday. As Briggs walked around the house, enjoying the graduation party and basking in the semifinal victory, he spied a gift he had acquired years ago. Hanging on the wall of his home was the jersey worn by the late Ted Marchell, a starting defenseman, in the 1976 title game, Cornell's overtime victory over Maryland. It was heavy red porthole mesh, with a white-stitched "Cornell" and "43" on the front and "43" on the back. Briggs removed it from its frame and tried it on. It fit perfectly.

As afternoon turned into evening on Saturday, Kirst and Wallace took a quick walk to a nearby convenience store to pick up gallons of bottled water and Gatorade. On the way back to the hotel, Kirst saw at a distance Mikey Powell, a four-time, first-team all-American attackman at Syracuse in the early 2000s. On this day, Powell was playing wall ball with his young daughter. Kirst and Wallace debated whether to say hello. Finally, curiosity won out—the two approached and introduced themselves. Powell recalled the night before the 2004 NCAA title game in Baltimore, his senior year, and preparing to face Navy. Powell said he typed a message and hand-delivered it to his teammates, sliding it under their hotel room doors at 3 a.m. The note told of his late grandfather, a horse trainer, and the grandfather's love for a horse nicknamed Number Nine. (Its real name was Love Potion Number Nine, after the famous 1963 hit song by The Searchers.) The Orange was going for NCAA title number nine, and the story of the underdog horse and its resilient efforts to win against all odds inspired Powell to center his message to his teammates around the horse, much beloved by his grandfather. The following day, before 43,898 fans, Powell's five assists helped Syracuse to a 14-13 victory. Powell was such a talent that after the game, the US Lacrosse Hall of Fame asked for his lacrosse gloves, so they could be displayed in its museum. As Kirst and Walker left Powell and headed back to the hotel, Kirst recalled a message his older brother Cole had sent months ago about another racehorse, Secretariat, and his record-breaking 1973 season, and the horse's unusual nickname.

On Saturday night, Cornell's players ventured around Patriot Place, grabbing fruit smoothies, signing autographs, and posing for pictures. Graham and Dalton, friends since grade nine, roommates for one last weekend, said they would never feel more cool or more important than they did in Foxborough. By Sunday morning, the attention turned to the title game and Maryland. The team had a quick film session before the offense walked to a practice field, secluded and protected from any prying eyes; the defense stayed in the hotel, working on schemes inside a ballroom and conference room. Toward the end of the afternoon, with dinner set for the same ballroom/conference room, Buczek sent a text message to the five captains. Which one of them wanted to address the team at the final team dinner of the 2025 season? All eyes fell on Kirst. "It was his team," says Kyle Smith. "He led us the whole year." Dinner that night was chicken parmesan and pasta and salad, the staple of the season. After dinner, their final official night as a team, hours before Cornell's biggest game in nearly fifty years, Kirst addressed his teammates, coaches, and staff members. Among his remarks, which he wrote down on a paper he sat on during dinner, was the racehorse Secretariat. In 1973, Secretariat won the famed Triple Crown—the Kentucky Derby, the Preakness Stakes, and the Belmont Stakes. His times at all three tracks are still course records. He was a dominant force, still much discussed and admired. Like the racehorse, Kirst said, Cornell had a chance the next day to win a triple crown—Ivy League regular season title, Ivy League tournament title, NCAA title. He then added something else about Secretariat. "His nickname," Kirst said, "was Big Red."

Later that night, in the same conference room as dinner, Cornell officials resumed their tradition of ordering late-night pizza, around 9 p.m., as a snack for any interested parties. Stevens, Wittink, and a few others walked into the conference room to grab a slice or two. Soon, Kirst joined the group, then several other seniors and super seniors. They discussed their favorite memories of the season and their careers, laughing and joking, reminiscing with pizza and water and Gatorade deep into the evening. "It was maybe my favorite moment of the whole season," says Wittink. In their hotel room that night, Dalton and Graham reflected on their years at Cornell and what lay ahead—Dalton had taken a job in finance in Toronto, and Graham had an extra year of eligibility, which he was spending at the University of Denver, as a grad student and attackman. The talk also turned to Monday's game. Historically, when Kirst had scored zero goals, he came back with a memorable performance. It happened his freshman year, 2022, when he was held without a goal in a loss in the Ivy League tournament, only to score seven goals in the next game, an NCAA first-round victory over Ohio State. In 2023, Army geared its defense to stopping Kirst, and he went without a goal. The following game against Brown he scored six goals in an easy victory. The 2024 season included a zero-goal performance in the season-ending loss to Penn. The next three games, albeit in the following season, Kirst scored six goals in all three. As they readied for bed and turned out the light on their time as roommates, Dalton and Graham had one final thought. "We both thought," Graham says now, "there's a really good chance CJ goes off tomorrow."

Monday morning, May 26, the day of the NCAA title game. Walker had spent the weekend reprising the quote from Dom Doria before the 2022 title game.

CHAPTER 8

When asked if he was ready to win the title, Doria responded, "I'm just ready for breakfast." It became a mantra again, though in some ways it had never left. Caddigan says when asked if he has weekend plans, he'll often respond, "I'm just focused on getting dinner." The delivery for Lizzio's tailgate party arrived in lot 3B, another truck full of subs and pasta and salad and meatballs. "The line for the concession stands in the quarterfinals and Final Four is a mile long," Lizzio says. "I just figured, let's take care of the food before and after the game, so we don't have to worry about it." Lohnes pressed several hundred pins, red with white letters, "WD > WS," with the NCAA title game teams and location around the rim. She pressed another series of buttons, also red with white letters, "Locked in." Among her takers was Michelle Kirst, CJ's mom. Around 11 a.m., two hours before the 1 p.m. face-off, the team left the Hilton Garden Inn Patriot Place and boarded its bus. The driver took the same route as before: a right turn onto an access road, past several businesses and a large movie theater, before turning right and passing lot 3B. Still hours before face-off, more than two thousand fans were already in place. The roar was even bigger than it had been on Saturday. After the bus passed, Kevin Moran was startled to see a former teammate who had flown in from Hong Kong. A younger Cornell alum, with a baby due in two weeks, arrived from Los Angeles, a day trip to see the title game.

Also in the crowd at lot 3B were Deborah and Mario Boiardi, George's parents. They send text messages to Buczek before most games, wishing the team luck. (He responds almost instantly.) This time they traveled from their house on Cape Cod to see the game in person. Wearing T-shirts with their son's 21 on the back, they did not particularly stand out because so many others donned apparel with the same number. "We had been there when Syracuse won [in 2009]," says Mario Boiardi. "And we wanted to be there again. We felt like something good was going to happen." As they walked through lot 3B with Teresa Rosenberger, the mother of one of George's Cornell teammates and close friends, Deborah remembers thinking of the Crescent Lot events when her son was playing and the fun they had with the parents of Tim DeBlois, a starting defenseman and close friend of their son, with Canadian kielbasa on the grill and beverages available out of the trunk of the DeBloises' car. "I remember thinking oh, I wish I could see the DeBlois family," Deborah says now. Within seconds, amid thousands of people, Karen DeBlois popped into view. She made a beeline for the Boiardis to give them a hug. Her husband, sitting under the shade of a tree like Ferdinand the Bull in the children's story, rose to join them.

In Cornell's locker room, the players went about their business as usual. This included the injured midfielder AJ Nikolic and his ritual of playing chess. Sheehan and Kirst passed the ball back and forth. Long steeled himself for one more game on his injured shoulder; he needed surgery, but that would wait until after

Memorial Day. The coaches had gone through Maryland's defensive personnel as best they could given the time constraints. Number 27 was Maryland's top defender, the Big Ten defenseman of the year. In the semifinal against Syracuse, he held quarterback Joey Spallina, wearing Mikey Powell's treasured number 22 jersey, without a point. (Spallina had an assist in the final seconds against Will Schaller's backup.) Longstick midfielder number 26 was everywhere; in the semifinal, AJ Larkin had two goals, three groundballs, and a caused turnover. Number 34 was a top shortstick defender; Geordy Holmes had two caused turnovers against Syracuse and played strong position defense, just like the other top shortstick, number 8, all-American Eric Kolar. A player Cornell did not need a refresher on was number 1, the goalie. They had seen him before, back in the 2022 title game, when Logan McNaney made seventeen saves and frustrated Kirst and Kelleher throughout Maryland's victory.

Around five minutes before 1 p.m., for one final time, Cornell left the locker room in its tight-twos, Kirst and Wallace leading from the front, sharing a fist bump before racing onto the field. The teams stood at attention for the national anthem, a giant American flag covering a good section of the field, just as it had in the photo Bozzi committed to memory, his motivation to return to this stage. Cornell reached the title game even though, in its quarterfinal and semifinal victories, Kirst shot a combined two for twenty, or 10 percent. The Big Red advanced with Cascadden's tireless work on face-offs and depth at shortstick defense, an advantage especially when playing two games in three days. The anthem over, the game was ready to start.

The teams faced each other at midfield. Referee Pete Buchanan told the teams, "What we do in life echoes in eternity." On the ESPN broadcast, Anish Shroff picked up that the quote was from the 2000 Ridley Scott movie *Gladiator*. Kirst and his seventy-six goals went to the offensive end, where he was guarded by Schaller. At the other end, Singer, the best on-ball defender, drew Maryland quarterback Braden Erksa. Staub drew Eric Spanos, a six-feet-four attackman with a rocket of an outside shot. Dooley drew lefty Daniel Kelly, a creative outside shooter.

The game began. Maryland's offense generated good shots, from Kelly and Spanos, Maryland's two leading goal scorers. Knust saved both, another strong start. At the other end, around four minutes into the game, Cornell inserted its second midfield—senior Ryan Sheehan, junior Brian Luzzi, and sophomore Ryan Waldman. Called "two Ryans and a Brian," the unit took shape early in the season, following the season-ending knee injury to Alex Holmes and the shift that pushed Dalton to the first line and bumped Sheehan to the second. Sheehan almost always drew the longstick. Waldman was a high-scoring attackman at Westfield (New Jersey) High—eighty points as a junior, sixty-nine as a senior—and now he was matched against a shortstick. Waldman dodged the shortstick defender and fired a lefty sidearm shot past McNaney. Opening goal to Cornell.

After Maryland tied the game, Cornell went back to its second midfield in the final minutes of the first quarter. Luzzi, on an off-ball cut, caught an inch-perfect pass from Long and fired a bounce shot past McNaney for a 2–1 lead. "It was a pretty standard play we had in for the title game," Luzzi says. "I wasn't even really expecting Mikey to throw me the ball. Then he gave me a perfect pass, and after I shot I didn't think it had gone in. I thought McNaney saved it. When I saw him turning around [to pick up the ball] I said wow, it went in." The Big Red had the lead, though Kirst had yet to score. In between the first and second quarters, Buczek told Kirst to calm down, to play his normal game. Early in the second quarter, with Cornell leading 3–2, Long broke his stick while trying to impede a defender from clearing the ball. As he raced off, Caddigan took his place, getting a couple treasured minutes in the national championship game. Soon after, Long was back on the field, jostled with a Maryland player for possession near the sideline and severely hurt his foot. He remained in the game, not telling anyone of the injury.

Late in the second quarter, Cornell led 5–4 when Kirst, scoreless since the quarterfinals, received the ball near the top of the offensive box. Dalton set a pick; the defenders hesitated, giving Kirst a step of freedom. Kirst fired an overhand lefty bounce shot that eluded McNaney with 1:49 left in the first half. Kirst scored his first goal since the final six minutes of the quarterfinal against Richmond, his first goal in 109 minutes 13 seconds, his first goal of 2025 Championship Weekend in Foxborough, his seventy-seventh of the season. Kirst accepted congratulations from his teammates, then looked toward the Cornell sidelines and nodded his head over and over. "That's the one that sticks with me," Sheehan says. "CJ's first goal, that high bouncer that wrapped around the crossbar. At that point I was like, alright, we're taking this thing. We're going to win this freaking game. CJ is always big on celebrations, and celebrates his friend's goals more than his own. When I saw how fired up he got after his goal, I knew it was huge." Maryland answered with a goal. In the final seconds of the first half, with Cornell leading 6–5, Knust traveled twenty yards out of the goal and bobbled a loose ball, then lost possession. It went to Spanos. With Knust far out of the goal and time about to expire, Spanos had an open goal at which to shoot. As he fired the ball, Dalton jumped and blocked the shot. The half ended with Cornell leading by a goal and Kirst, finally, on the scoresheet.

Five minutes into the third quarter, Kirst again received a pick from Dalton, giving him a step on Schaller, and he scored on a close shot for a 7–5 lead and goal number seventy-eight. Minutes later, Kirst found himself matched against reserve Jack McDonald. Free from Schaller for once, he didn't hesitate to go to the goal and scored for an 8–5 lead. Maryland scored, and had an ensuing possession, when TJ Lamb forced a turnover and cleared the ball. Kirst again got the ball and found himself matched against senior Colin Burlace, not Schaller. Kirst went to the cage and scored his fourth consecutive goal, all unassisted. The Big Red led 9–6, and in the ESPN broadcast, Shroff said, "This is what greatness is all about." Less than three minutes remained in the third quarter. At the end of the quarter, Cornell led 9–7. ESPN's Dana Boyle asked Buczek what his team needed to do to win its first title since 1977. "We've got to finish with our heart," he said. "Cornell-like effort, George Boiardi-like effort. That's going to allow us to push this thing over the top."

The Boiardi-like effort came almost instantly. Maryland had possession, attempting to go from defense to offense. Kirst and Goldstein pressured the defenders—Long, hampered by his foot injury, provided brief resistance. A long clearing pass went astray. Kirst grabbed the loose ball and fed Goldstein, who scored on a rocket of a nondominant, left-handed shot for a 10–7 lead. Two goals from Maryland cut the deficit to 10–9 with 9:23 remaining. The Terrapins won the ensuing face-off and sent out their starting midfield. Cornell countered with junior longstick defender Eddie Rayhill and, at shortstick, Lamb and Box. Maryland worked the ball to Spanos, its leading scorer; his low-to-low shot was saved by Knust. Cornell cleared the ball with 8:15 to play but lost possession. Maryland began its march from defense to offense with the ball in the stick of Schaller. At the other end of the field was the chance to tie the game. Schaller saw Kolar, his teammate at Hill School in Pottstown, Pennsylvania, about ten yards away, just across the midfield line. Schaller threw a looping pass. Kolar, staring into the sun, never moved his stick. The ball landed behind him, then bounced out of bounds. Turnover Maryland. Cornell had the ball back. And, because Schaller was clearing up the right side of the field, he was nowhere near Kirst when play restarted. Kirst recognized this as well. He asked for the ball behind the goal, then drove against graduate student Jackson Canfield, got past Canfield, and scored on a point-blank shot. His fifth goal of the game gave Cornell an 11–9 lead with 6:42 to play.

Maryland inserted freshman Peter Laake into the lineup, replacing Canfield. Laake went to cover Goldstein. Cornell gained possession, and McNaney saved a close shot from Long. On the clearing attempt, a Maryland player jumped offside. The ball went back to Cornell. Goldstein raced past Laake and scored on a close shot for a 12–9 lead with 4:08 to play. Maryland, leading the nation in clearing percentage at 91 percent, had failed on three consecutive crucial clears. At this point, on the jubilant sideline, Caddigan turned to sophomore Anthony Bartolotto. "I said, 'Dude, we're going to win the natty!'" says Caddigan, a reference to the national title. "And he looked at me and said, 'Dude, shut the hell up! It's not over yet!'"

Maryland closed to 12–10 on a goal by senior Zach Whittier, a speedy midfielder from Kensington, Maryland, with 1:22 to play. Freshman Michael Melkonian won the ensuing face-off, with Staub picking up the loose ball, and Buczek called a time-out an instant before Staub lost possession. On the restart, with 1:08 to play, Maryland went into desperation mode. It double-teamed Kirst, hoping for a result similar to the regular-season game against Penn State, when the defenders forced Kirst out of bounds to regain possession. This time Kirst raced around both players and scored into an empty net. The Big Red led 13–10. Kirst ran to the large section of Cornell fans and pointed toward his mother and brothers sitting there. It was his eighty-second goal of the season, tying an NCAA single-season record. More important by far, it gave Cornell an insurmountable lead with fifty seconds to play. As the goal went in, Bartolotto turned to Caddigan: "'Holy shit, we're going to win this!' And I told him yeah, that's what I've been saying!"

Sheehan, the coach's son, took nothing for granted. "Guys started unbuckling their helmets, getting ready to throw them in the air, and I remember freaking out," Sheehan says. "I was like guys, it's not over yet! Looking back on it, I'm thinking, wow I was being a loser." Sheehan estimates he attended at least fifteen Championship Weekends as a fan, many to watch his father's LeMoyne team play for the Division II national title. (The Dolphins won six times and lost four.) "Ever since I could actually understand the sport," he says, "that moment where the guys throw their equipment and storm the field gives me chills, every time." With three seconds left, the ball wound up in Knust's stick. It was over. Cornell's players stormed the field, Sheehan getting to participate in the event he had seen countless times from the stands and dreamed about even more often. "Racing onto the field," Sheehan says, "is the coolest thing I'll ever do in my life, until I get married and have kids." Daniel Murphy, photographing the game for *The Boston Globe*, caught the players from the sideline racing onto the field, released like souls from Hades, to form a dog pile on top of Knust, the traditional postgame greeting of the goalie that, in this case, was forty-eight years in the making. At the front were defensive midfielders Gilmartin and Box, with Firth in between. On the sideline, as the injured players lumbered to join their teammates, an NCAA official handed them the mahogany-and-gold trophy. Seniors Alex Holmes and Antonio Topouzis and junior AJ Nikolic were the first to take hold of the treasured hardware.

Kirst finally took off his right lacrosse glove, revealing a massive tape job on his right hand, with the hard shell protecting it. The players celebrated briefly on the field before going back to the sideline for a huddle around the coaches, then the traditional postgame handshake. On their way to the huddle, Kelleher and Dalton noticed Long on all fours, sick to his stomach. In the chaos they called for a trainer; no one heard, so they shouted louder. Long's foot injury, combined with his existing shoulder injury, had left him wracked with pain. Finally the trainer arrived. "I was throwing up for two minutes, I felt like I was dying," Long says. "With the dog pile, no one saw me off to the side. You know once you're sick and get it all out, you feel jazzed up? That's what happened. Danielle [Hemly, the trainer] came over and said, you gotta stay down. And by then I felt better. I said, 'Danielle, we did it!' And went over to the section of Cornell fans."

In the huddle immediately after the game, Wittink remembers one of the first things Buczek told the players: "You made Tom Howley a national champion." Kirst went to each teammate, and to his family in the stands, saying the same refrain: We did it. We did it. "He must've said it a hundred times," says Bozzi. "That day was amazing. I remember it minute by minute." Added Smith, "CJ went through a lot of pain every day. At practice he was still the best player, he was by far the hardest worker. You couldn't tell he had a hand injury. No matter his circumstance, he just wanted to get better. He toughed it out." Wittink, watching every game from the sideline, says he paid particular attention to Kirst and his right hand. "The entire season," Wittink says, "I don't think I saw one defender, one opposing team, target his hand or go after him. Maybe it was a sign that they knew he was something special."

Goldstein finished the title game with four goals. His speed gave Maryland fits. McNaney, one of the best goalkeepers in recent memory, never made a save on Goldstein. Goldstein's father had been on the short end of Cornell title games in 1987 and 1988. Same with Steve Long in the 1987 title game and Mikey Long with two assists in the championship. Knust, once so overlooked he did not play in an intrasquad scrimmage, finished the title game with twelve saves.

The team, after the handshake with Maryland's players, cut down the white net from both lacrosse goals, hugged family and friends in the stands, then went into the locker room and launched into their victory song: "Hurricane" by Bob Dylan, a tradition going back decades, one of several post-victory rituals. They posed for pictures with the trophy, quickly showered, and boarded the bus to parking lot 3B. En route, Buczek turned to Stevens and said, "Thank God we lost to Penn State [in the regular season]." "We needed a wake-up call," Stevens says. "We needed that failure to guide us, so we re-understood the level of commitment needed. If you look at Jack Cascadden after that game, in every fourth quarter it felt like not only did he win his matchup, he dominated it. It's the underlying theme from the fall, and from losing to Penn State. To win a championship, you have to fail, you have to be pushed outside your comfort zone."

The party had truly started; thousands of Cornell fans stayed behind to celebrate. When Kirst walked off the bus with the trophy, he saw a group of seniors from the 2022 season. "You guys taught me everything," he shouted to them.

"You're the reason I'm holding this trophy." Kirst shared the trophy with them, and they accepted it, beer in one hand, the trophy in the other, tears of joy rolling down their faces. Longstick midfielder Duke Reeder, the transfer from Stanford, ran into a Cornell lacrosse friend from back home in San Francisco. "I've never seen him so happy," Reeder said of Roy Lang, at the center of so much of the drama in the last-second loss in the 2009 title game, now joyously celebrating the end of a forty-eight-year drought.

Nearby, the food from Pulcinella's was still going strong. Beth, the manager, proudly wore her "Big Red 15" T-shirt as she oversaw the proceedings, pausing only briefly to take a picture with Lizzio and Cascadden. Michelle Kirst entered parking lot 3B wearing both of Lohnes's spirit pins—and a little bit of a frown. She worried her son's final goal into the empty net had been poor sportsmanship. Mike Levine, attackman at Cornell in the mid-1990s, known during the week as a high-profile sports executive and agent and on lacrosse weekends by his nickname Vino, had a quick response. "She came over and said, 'Vino, do you think CJ will get in trouble for shooting into the empty goal? My husband would be turning over in his grave.' And I told her, your husband would be happy his son scored such an important goal. It wasn't bad sportsmanship. The game wasn't over yet. It was pretty amazing her first reaction was to be worried about sportsmanship and whether her son did the right thing. It shows what kind of person she is, and the selflessness with which she raised those boys." Maryland Coach John Tillman agreed. "We did not think it was running up the score at all," he said. "That's more about who Michelle Kirst is."

The trophy careened from one group to the next, much as it had after the first NCAA title game, Cornell over Maryland in 1971, when Richie Moran brought it to his favorite bar, The Waltz Inn in Stuart Manor, near Hofstra Stadium. Now, the trophy made its way to Deborah and Mario Boiardi; they were asked if they wanted to hold it. No, Mario politely said, it's not our trophy. The fan insisted. The Boiardis held the trophy while someone snapped a picture and posted it on social media. It received thousands of likes and comments. "If I had known they were going to take my picture," Deborah quipped, "I would have gotten my hair done." Several players, when asked their favorite memory of the day, mentioned the picture of the Boiardis. Many Cornell players and fans printed out the picture as a keepsake. After all, it had been twenty-one years since George died, his jersey was number 21, and in that twenty-first year, Cornell won the Ivy League regular season title, the Ivy League tournament title, and the NCAA title; also, Landon School, Boiardi's high school alma mater, won the Interstate Athletic Conference regular season title and IAC tournament. The 21 year was a clean sweep.

Teddy Lamade, Boiardi's classmate and teammate in twelve sports seasons at Landon, watched the title game on TV from his home outside the nation's capital.

He was struck by Buczek's remarks at the end of the third quarter, that winning the game would take a "Boiardi-like effort." Kirst, too, in his postgame comments to Dana Boyle, said, "Coach Moran, George Boiardi, this is all for them." Lamade still talks about his close friend Boiardi, especially to his two sons. He says when his younger son does something untoward, or something that needs correcting, Lamade gives him a look. "I don't even say anything. I give him a look," Lamade says, "and he says, 'I know, I know, George wouldn't have done that.'" Lamade estimates that among his Landon classmates and teammates and friends, there are fifteen sons or nephews named George. Recently, one member of the friend group sent out an exhortation: "He said, 'Guys, six more and we get to 21! Let's get there! I know we can do it!'" Lamade is a little more circumspect. "Some of us are in our forties," he says. "I think it'll have to be from the next generation. But we'll get there."

By this time, Andy Phillips, head of the Cornell Lacrosse Association, was leaving lot 3B and heading home, driving back to Manhasset through Memorial Day traffic to let out Griz and watch the replay of the title game. Behind the wheel of his car, he began formulating the email he would send to five people: Dave Pietramala, Jeff Tambroni, Ben DeLuca, Matt Kerwick, and Peter Milliman. They are the five remaining Cornell coaches who steered the ship during the drought. "I wanted to say thank you," Phillips says. "This title was fifty years in the making, and every one of them was part of that fifty years, was part of that foundation. I pointed out specific milestones each of them achieved at Cornell. . . . One thing I told all of them. I said, 'Your contingent showed up. Players from your era, players you coached, showed up. If nothing else, you should consider that your proudest achievement. You coached a group of players who must've had a good experience, because they continue to show up for Cornell."

Away from parking lot 3B, Buck Briggs lingered in Gillette Stadium a little longer. It was a beautiful day, sunny and warm, and he was in no rush to leave the historic moment. Briggs was close friends with Bob Buhmann, mercurial Cornell goalie, star of the 1971 NCAA title game, his 22 saves that day a remarkable achievement in any circumstance, made more so by Buhmann's backup status for much of the year, his sudden thrust into the lineup when the starter was injured in early May, and by Buhmann's lifelong bouts with epilepsy. Briggs sat in the stands as an undergrad for the glory days of Mike French and Eamon McEneaney. He skipped his own graduation to attend the 1976 title game at Brown Stadium, Cornell over Maryland by three goals on a perfect New England early summer afternoon. As a grad student in Washington, DC, he had an easier drive than most Cornell faithful to the 1977 title game in Charlottesville, the searing day when McEneaney roasted the Blue Jays with three goals and five assists. In 1978, Briggs was in Boston for a wedding and missed the title game at Rutgers

Stadium. He remembers opening the newspaper the next morning and seeing the final score, in tiny eight-point agate type, hardly appropriate for the life-altering message it conveyed: "Johns Hopkins 13, Cornell 8." Seeking confirmation, Briggs found a story in *The Boston Globe* with the following lede: "Cornell's record went that-a-way in Piscataway." The formidable forty-two-game winning streak was over. The frustrating forty-eight-year title drought began. Briggs moved around the East Coast. He went from working for the NFL Players Association to working for the NFL, also teaching classes at Cornell and Penn—always Penn in the fall, Cornell in the spring, to coincide with lacrosse. Briggs hosted the team and coaches at the Old Stone Heap. He drove Buhmann's beat-up pickup truck on errands around the property, the truck Buhmann gifted shortly before he died of brain cancer in 2016. Months later, Briggs graciously accepted when someone offered him the jersey Ithaca native Ted Marchell wore in the 1976 title game, a starting defenseman in one of the great days in Cornell's athletic history. It was the same jersey Marchell wore in his obituary photo, after his death following a sudden illness, also in 2016.

Inside empty Gillette Stadium, Briggs resumed his lap around the concourse level. He walked past the workers and the drone of their leaf blowers as they collected trash into piles. He walked above where Cornell's joyous players had formed their dog pile after winning the title; he rounded the corner into the far end zone, and the goal where, in the final seconds in the 2009 championship, Syracuse tied the game against Cornell, then, minutes later, scored the winning goal. Briggs kept walking, finding himself at the top of section 117, filled on Memorial Days 2009 and 2025 with Cornell fans of all ages, screaming and hoping and wishing and cheering and praying and, ultimately, crying, once tears of heartbreak, now tears of joy. The red and white confetti on the field lifted and fell with a soft breeze. The shadows were growing longer; the day was nearly done. On the field below were the lacrosse goals without nets, cut down as part of the traditional celebration by the winning team, which for the first time since 1977 was Briggs's team. Behind him was a giant scoreboard that told the story, Cornell over Maryland by three goals on a perfect New England early summer afternoon. Briggs took in the scene, forty-eight years in the making—one that, as Kirst noted, included so many absent friends, including the one Briggs carried on his back and another in his heart. Briggs took one last look, then turned around and slipped quietly out of the stadium.

Epilogue

After a few hours in parking lot 3B, the Cornell coaches, players, and staff boarded the team bus back to Ithaca, seniors in the back, juniors and sophomores in the middle, freshmen in the front. Around midnight, as the team entered New York state, it received a police escort. When the bus pulled into Schoellkopf Field's parking lot, the police officers asked for pictures and autographs. From there, the players and the trophy went to the house in Collegetown of several of the juniors. The following afternoon, the seniors graduated in a quickly arranged ceremony. Most of the students had gone home; still, around one thousand people from Ithaca attended. LaFalce remembers his young son asking for, and receiving, several player autographs, with Kirst taking the time to sign every slip of paper and pose for every picture.

The end, when it arrived, came quickly. A couple days after the title game, eight seniors traveled to Europe for a prearranged graduation trip. Kirst and his family and several teammates traveled to Washington, DC, where he won the Tewaaraton Award as the nation's top men's player. It culminated a season in which he finished with eighty-two goals, thirty-three assists, forty-three groundballs, and nineteen caused turnovers. The caused turnovers tied Dooley for the team high, a remarkable achievement for an attackman. The all-around excellence caught the eye of one Cornell alum in particular. "CJ Kirst was way more than goals and assists," says Maryland Coach John Tillman, a 1991 Cornell graduate. "It was also his energy and leadership and passion. He was able to lift everyone around him. That's what great players do. . . . I'm a huge fan of the joy he plays with. I was good friends with his dad, and you see a lot of his dad in CJ. Kyle was a guy who loved lacrosse and loved people. He had a huge heart. He loved the game, and all his kids love the game. That's a credit to him and Michelle. If you're a young player, and you want to watch how to play the game, put on some film and watch CJ. He'll show you."

After the Tewaaraton ceremony, Kirst prepared for surgery on his right hand and a seven-week recovery. Long prepared for surgery on his shoulder, also with a recovery period of several weeks. Wallace packed his bags and headed to the University of Virginia, where he enrolled in grad school and joined the school's nationally ranked football team as a tight end. Wallace changed schools and changed sports, but the background on his smartphone remained the photo of Boiardi's locker, taken years ago, on the first day Wallace entered the locker room as a freshman. Singer, too, enrolled in grad school at Elon University in North Carolina and played linebacker on the school's football team. Kyle Smith, set to begin his job with a defense contractor in Boston right after the title game, asked to push his start date back a week, explaining the unusual circumstances. His request was granted. Chris Davis, who once confided in friends that he believed his career was over, whose back pain was so significant he could barely walk, signed up for an ultramarathon. Jordan Stevens stepped aside from coaching; he and his young family were moving to Philadelphia, and he was taking a white-collar job for a recruiting firm. "I'm going to miss the hell out of it," he says. "It doesn't mean I love Cornell any less."

In early June, the Cornell class of 1980 was on campus for its forty-fifth reunion. Jarett Wait, Cornell alum, parent of a former Cornell lacrosse player, said one gathering featured Stevens walking in with the NCAA trophy. Wait was among the dozens and dozens of attendees who yanked out their phones to film the proceedings. Wait then joined his classmates in line to pose for a picture with the trophy. Wait had already done as much back in Gillette Stadium's parking lot 3B, but as he says, one can never have too much documentation of such events.

Deborah and Mario Boiardi returned to their home in Massachusetts and hosted their five grandchildren, all boys, including one named George. In the late summer, Deborah Boiardi suffered a leg injury outside the house. The full recovery took several weeks. "I was sitting around like a loaf," she says. "It really shined the light on things I want to do in the future. I want to be more involved again, to get back on my feet and take more walks and volunteer more." Mario Boiardi stays fit with 8 a.m. swims in the Atlantic Ocean. He recently bought a wetsuit for the occasions. Their son's story was back in the news in early January 2023, after Buffalo Bills safety Damar Hamlin collided with a Cincinnati Bengals wide receiver and collapsed. His heartbeat had to be restored on the field, and he spent several days in a local hospital in critical condition. Hamlin is believed to have suffered from commotio cordis, Latin for "a disruption of the heart." The American Heart Association estimates there are around thirty cases in the United States each year. It is a rare cardiac event affecting athletes in high-impact sports and believed to be related to Boiardi's cause of death. Hamlin made a full recovery, so much so that the following year he played in fourteen of the team's seventeen regular-season games.

On April 16, 2021, Loyola Blakefield freshman defenseman Peter Laake was struck by the ball in his chest and collapsed during a game in Baltimore. He was revived by CPR and an automated external defibrillator (AED) at the stadium. His recovery was such that he spent two weeks in the hospital and, within three weeks, was back on the field. On Memorial Day 2025 he was in Foxborough, Massachusetts, playing as a reserve defenseman for Maryland against Cornell. In a way this, too, is another of Boiardi's lasting legacies, as described by Cornell's Julie Greco: "In the Cornell community, Boiardi's legacy lives on in several ways, with the most visible being the increase of automated external defibrillator machines on campus. While there was an AED on the field the day Boiardi died, the university made a commitment to increase the number of machines available. Within ten years of his death, there were one hundred and seventy-three on campus, many of which are hardwired to Cornell dispatch and emergency services." JR Bordley, Boiardi's classmate and close friend at Landon, is a teacher and assistant lacrosse coach at Landon. He says the Hamlin and Laake incidents struck a chord. "The brilliance of the doctors saved Damar Hamlin and saved Peter Laake," he says, "but I like to think they're also alive because of George."

Buczek went to South Korea with the US under-twenty lacrosse team, which won the silver medal in the 2025 World Championship. He returned home and got married to the former Madeline Keip in Trumansburg, New York. In late September, on the weekend the lacrosse team received its national title rings, Buczek took part in the annual golf tournament. He hit a hole in one. Buczek also, intentionally, ordered one ring too many. He brought the extra with him to Bethesda, Maryland, in mid-October. He had accepted the invitation from Landon School to speak at the annual George Boiardi Forum for Ethical Reflection. He made his remarks to Landon's lower school, middle school, and high school students, plus Deborah and Mario Boiardi, one of their daughters and her family, and many friends of Boiardi's from his Landon and Cornell days. Buczek shared how Boiardi remains so important to the Cornell program and the tangible ways they honor him and seek to emulate the example he set. He discussed what it means to be a good teammate and a good friend. He received a standing ovation. After Buczek answered a series of questions—from a fourth grader, an eighth grader, and two high schoolers—the students returned to class, and Buczek posed for pictures with Boiardi's family and friends. In some of the pictures,

Deborah can be seen holding the 2025 Cornell lacrosse national title ring that, hours earlier, Buczek had given the Boiardi family.

George Boiardi is buried in a cemetery atop a hill in Georgetown. It is secluded and peaceful, trees swishing in a soft breeze on a mid-October afternoon, sunny and surprisingly mild. At the top of his tombstone is his full name, then it mentions he was a beloved son, brother, and friend. Toward the bottom is an excerpt from the poem "To an Athlete Dying Young," by A. E. Housman. The line reads, "Smart lad, to slip betimes away / From fields where glory does not stay." In the middle of Boiardi's tombstone is this: "Captain, Cornell University Lacrosse." There is no date, because none is needed. He is as much a leader now as he was in his playing days.

Acknowledgments

This book would not have been possible without many people. First is Jane Bunker, director of Cornell University Press. She and I started light discussions for a book on Cornell's 2025 season during the quarterfinals—knowing it is bad luck to plan such things before they happen, I assure those of a superstitious bent reading this that our discussions were very theoretical. After Cornell won the championship on Memorial Day evening, probably around the time the party in lot 3B was slowing down, Jane and I had a longer talk. In early July, the project moved forward in earnest. Jane provided leadership, vision, and a sympathetic ear as the book took shape quickly. Jane was the CJ Kirst of this endeavor, with backbone, confidence, and excellence on many fronts. She also encouraged me to extend the book's boundaries beyond the 2025 season and into the title drought, the 2020 canceled season, the pandemic, and the blight of early recruiting.

India Miraglia from the acquisitions team was Ryan Goldstein, with excellence beyond her youth and good ideas to reshape the book and make it stronger, an awesome complement to Jane. One of the great joys of writing the 2022 book *We Showed Baltimore: The Lacrosse Revolution of the 1970s and Richie Moran's Big Red* was working with the Three Hills / Cornell Press folks, especially Michael McGandy, with his aversion to starting sentences with *but* and for whom a chronological narrative was the best way—lessons I used for this book as well. The first book also put me in touch with so many helpful and wonderful Cornell people. Jarett Wait, Cornell alum, father of a Cornell lacrosse alum, was a tremendous interview, an amazing resource of photos and videos from the season, and an inspiration of energy and optimism that could rival CJ Kirst. His text messages and insights during the 2025 season formed the nucleus of this book. Buck Briggs was immensely helpful with both books, with his keen observations, brilliant intellect, and gracious willingness to make introductions on my behalf. He opens more doors than a hotel doorman. I ended the book with him because he was the personification of the forty-eight-year title drought. Jordan Stevens, in the midst of moving from Ithaca to Philadelphia, starting a new job, and being a father and husband to his young family and son TJ, gave me two lengthy interviews, countless observations, and contact information for many of the seniors and super seniors. (For players on the current roster, I went through Jeremy Hartigan and Shawn Gillen from Cornell Sports Information, both of whom answered my questions quickly despite having many projects on their plate.)

ACKNOWLEDGMENTS

Andy Phillips, on both books, was a feeder like Tim Goldstein, providing helpful contact information for any number of Cornell lacrosse alumni at all hours of the day and night. I thought I knew a lot about lacrosse until I came into contact with both Andy and Howard Borkan; it is very humbling to be around people who know so much and are so kind to share that knowledge. If I ever write another lacrosse book, and I very, very much want to do so, I will lean heavily on Howard's keen eye and remarkable memory. At the very least, I am hopeful my constant entreaties to him are less painful than his professed love of the NFL's New York Jets.

I spoke to all but one of Cornell's seniors and super seniors, plus several players back for the 2026 season. I enjoyed every single minute of those interviews. I found the players to be honest, self-deprecating, and willing to tell me things on any number of topics, some of them rather sensitive. It was humbling to receive so many life lessons from people aged eighteen to twenty-two or, for the super seniors, aged twenty-three. My goals for the book were one, make it accurate and as behind-the-scenes as I could; two, make it something the players would want to show their family; and three, make it something from which a young player or even a young athlete might benefit. With this I had in mind my nieces and nephews: William, a freshman defenseman on the lacrosse team at Skidmore College, and a proud alum of Gonzaga College High School and Northfield Mount Hermon School as a postgrad; Robert, in middle school and an active participant in Gunston Soccer Club in Alexandria, Virginia; and Walker, in fourth grade at Little Flower School, with attendant membership in Maplewood football and the Bethesda Lacrosse Club. Also my beloved nieces, Charlotte, a senior and captain for the Stone Ridge School of the Sacred Heart swim team in Bethesda, Maryland; and Beatrice, a freshman in the marching band and set to join crew at West Potomac High School in Alexandria.

A huge tip of the cap to my colleagues in the lacrosse media. Terry Foy, Matt Kinnear, Kevin Brown, Dan Aburn and all my friends at *Inside Lacrosse* who love the sport and have put up with me since 2003; the good people at *Lacrosse Magazine*, where I began my lacrosse journalism career in 1991; my editors at *The Washington Post*, where I spent twenty years and learned so much; and my current colleagues at EWTN, the Global Catholic TV Network. It is perhaps fitting that I love so much a sport that was given its name by French Jesuit priests, is named for the accoutrement of a Catholic bishop, and even has a patron saint. Last, thank you to my mom and my siblings for providing constant inspiration and support and patience and friendship. I need every bit of it.

www.ingramcontent.com/pod-product-compliance
Lightning Source LLC
Chambersburg PA
CBHW020649060526
44446CB00041B/340/J